CW01676944

Reiki Evolution

The Orange Book – a collection

by Taggart King

www.reiki-evolution.co.uk
Email: taggart@reiki-evolution.co.uk

18 ARTICLES ABOUT REIKI

About this book

This book takes as its starting point six year's of articles written by Taggart King for the Reiki Evolution e-mail newsletter which, as of Spring 2007, was being sent to a list of 13,000 subscribers.

Taggart has selected eighteen articles and worked through each one again, updating, rewriting and extending its coverage where necessary, and you will find running through these articles a vision of Reiki as a simple and powerful self-development tool and treatment method, free from the clutter, busyness and dogma of Western Reiki practice.

Taggart roots his vision of Reiki in the original practices of Mikao Usui, Reiki's founder, and he emphasises the need for simplicity, personal dedication and commitment in obtaining the many benefits that are available to the student through Reiki.

The articles that Taggart has written fall comfortably into two themes:

1. Reiki fundamentals
2. Developing yourself further

Though you could see these two categories as corresponding to the two Reiki levels (First Degree and Second Degree) we suggest that all the articles will be of interest to and of benefit to all Reiki people at whatever Reiki level.

We suggest that to gain the greatest benefit from this collection of essays, you should not read the whole volume through all in one go.

Take your time to work through the essays; there's no rush!

Read one essay every few days and ponder its contents. Think about your own practice of Reiki and consider whether what you have read has helped in some way:

- Have some of your questions been answered?
- Do you now have further questions?
- Are you prompted to try something in a different way?
- Are you prompted to add something to your practice?
- Are you prompted to eliminate something from your practice?

This book is not just a collection of essays: this is a practical workbook. And to help the reader to gain the most out of this book, we have allowed ample room in this volume for notes to be made, so the reader can add their own thoughts, questions and conclusions to the text.

We hope that these articles make a difference to you and that your practice of Reiki is enhanced as a result.

With best wishes,

Taggart King
Reiki Evolution

5 Rose Lane, Pinchbeck, Spalding, Lincolnshire PE11 3RN
Web: www.reiki-evolution.co.uk
eMail; taggart@reiki-evolution.co.uk

Fundamentals

初傳

This section begins with a summary of the basic practices and principles of Reiki First Degree.

Next we examine important aspects of the practice of Reiki, applicable to all Reiki levels; for example, we consider Mikao Usui's precepts, the meditative practice of mindfulness, and the role of compassion in Usui's system.

Then we move on to consider your Reiki development, the best state of mind to cultivate when practising Reiki, and we consider the sensations that you might experience when practising Reiki, and what to make of them.

Finally, we deal with the various restrictions that some teachers have decided to impose on Reiki, and discuss the nature of the energy, intelligent or otherwise.

Here are the articles, together with the dates when the original versions of the articles were published in the Reiki Evolution eZine.

May 2005	Back to Basics: Reiki First Degree
Aug 2004	The Precepts
Feb 2004	Mindfulness and Compassion
May 2003	The Kaizen of Reiki
Nov 2005	Get out of the way!
Feb 2006	Reiki Sensations
May 2002	Restrictions on Reiki
Aug 2001	Intelligent Energy?

Back to Basics: Reiki First Degree

May 2005

People end up on First Degree courses for many reasons and come from an amazing variety of backgrounds, all attending for their own personal reasons. Reiki courses in the UK present a whole variety of approaches, some "traditional" Western-style, some more Japanese in content, some wildly different and almost unrecognisable, some free and intuitive, others dogmatic and based on rules about what you should always do and not do. Reiki is taught in so many ways, and students will tend to imagine that the way that they were taught is the way that Reiki is taught and practised by most other Reiki people.

What I have tried to do in this article is to present a simple guide to the essence of First Degree: what it's all about and what we should be doing and thinking about to get the most out of our experience of Reiki at this level. My words are addressed to anyone at First Degree level, or anyone who would like to review the essence of First Degree.

First Degree is all about connecting to the energy, learning to develop your sensitivity to the flow of energy, working on yourself to develop your ability as a channel and to enhance self-healing, and working on other people. There are many approaches to doing these things, and I wanted below to touch on each area and to dispel some myths that may have been passed on.

Connecting to the energy

On your Reiki course you will have received some attunements or some empowerments. Attunements are not standard rituals within the world of Reiki and take many forms, some simpler and some more complex. They have evolved and changed greatly during their journey from teacher to teacher in the West. There is no "right way" to carry out an attunement and the individual details of a ritual do not matter a great deal. They all work. Equally, there is no "correct" number of attunements that have to be carried out at First Degree level. The number four is quoted often as being the "correct" number but this has no basis in Reiki's original form, and whether you receive one, two, three or four rituals on your course, that is fine.

On your course you may have received some "empowerments" rather than attunements, though these are less common. The word "empowerment", or "Reiju empowerment", refers to a connection ritual that has come to us from some Japanese sources, and is closer in essence to the empowerment that Mikao Usui conveyed to his students. Again, there is no correct number of empowerments that has to be carried out. One is enough but it is nice to do more.

What we experience when receiving an attunement or an empowerment will vary a lot. Some people have fireworks and bells and whistles and that's nice for them; other people notice a lot less, very little, or even nothing, and that's fine too. What we feel when we have an attunement is not a guide to how well it has worked for us. Attunements work, and sometimes we will have a strong experience, but it's not compulsory! Whether we have noticed a lot, or very little, the attunement will have given us what we need.

Since in Mikao Usui's system you would have received empowerments from him again and again, it would be nice if you could echo this practice by receiving further empowerments (or attunements) and perhaps these might be available at your teacher's Reiki shares or get-togethers, if they hold them. But it is possible to receive distant Reiju empowerments and various teachers make them freely available as a regular 'broadcast'. This is not essential, and your connection to Reiki once given does not fizzle out, but it would be a beneficial practice if you could receive regular empowerments from someone.

Developing your Sensitivity to the energy

People's experience of energy when they first start working with Reiki can vary. Some people notice more than others, particularly in the early stages, and if we perhaps notice less going on in our hands when compared with another student on the course we can become disillusioned to an extent: that little voice in your head says "I know Reiki works for everyone... but it's not going to work for me. I knew it wasn't going to work for me". Well if this describes your situation then I can say to you that Reiki will work for you, and is working for you, and the vast majority of Reiki people can feel the flow of energy through them in some way, though your particular 'style' of sensing the energy may not involve the more usual heat, fizzing, tingling, pulsing etc. that many people experience. There are a few Reiki Master/Teachers out there who feel absolutely nothing in their hands, but this is not common, and Reiki is still working for them.

Sensitivity to the flow of energy develops over time, with practice. Some people are lucky enough to be able to feel quite a lot in their hands and in their bodies to begin with, but others have to be patient, trust that Reiki is working for them, and perhaps focus more on the feedback that they receive from the people that they treat, rather than what they feel – or don't feel – in their hands.

It would be worthwhile if all First Degree students spent some time regularly practising feeling energy: between your hands, around your cat or dog or your pot plant or a tree, around someone else's head and shoulders, over someone's supine body, noticing any differences in the sensation in your hands as you move your hands from one place to another. Don't expect to experience a particular thing or a particular intensity of feeling. Be neutral and simply notice what experience you have and how that experience might change from one area to another.

On some First Degree courses this process will be taught as "scanning", where you hover your hands over the recipient's body, drift your hands from one place to another, and notice any areas which are drawing more energy. This can provide some useful information in terms of suggesting additional or alternative hand-positions to use when you treat, and can suggest areas where you are going to spend longer when you treat.

Working on yourself

It is vital that after going on a First Degree course you establish a regular routine of working on yourself in order to develop your fledgling ability as a channel and to obtain the benefits that Reiki can provide in terms of balancing your life and self-healing. Most people decide to learn Reiki because they are looking for some personal benefits as well as looking to help other people, and the way to get the most out of the Reiki system is to work on yourself regularly.

On your First Degree course you will have been taught a self-treatment method, perhaps a Japanese-style meditation but more likely the Western "hands-on" self-treatment method. You will most likely have been given a set of hand-positions to use, but please remember that these positions are not set in stone and, particularly if some of the hand positions are quite uncomfortable to use in practice, you will develop your own style. It is fine to change the hand positions based on what feels right from one self-treatment to another, and you should do what feels appropriate. There is no "correct" set of positions that you have to use, and each hand-position does not have to be held for a particular period of time. Treat for however long you have time for, and however long feels right for each hand-position you decide to use.

Many people are taught that they have to do a "21 day self-treat", and some people have the impression that they then do not need to self-treat any more. The "21 day" period has no real basis, and I can say that you ought to be thinking in terms of working on yourself long-term. To gain the greatest benefits from this wonderful system you need to persevere and make working with energy a permanent feature of your life with Reiki, a basic background practice, the effects of which will build up cumulatively as you continue to work with the energy.

You may have been taught a series of energy exercises and meditations called "Hatsurei ho" which comes from Japanese Reiki, and I can commend this practice to you. It is a wonderful way of grounding, balancing, and enhancing you ability as a channel, and should be a regular part of your Reiki routine.

Treating other people

First Degree is also about starting to work on other people, a process which also benefits the giver, so plus points all round really! A few students may have been taught not to treat others at First Degree, or for a particular prescribed period, but this is an unnecessary restriction and Reiki can be shared with other people straight away.

There are many different approaches to treating others, and we should not get bogged down with too many rules and regulations about how we 'must' proceed. Reiki can be approached in quite a regimented way in some lineages, and students may worry that if they are not remembering all the stages that they 'have' to carry out then they will not be carrying out the treatment properly. This is an unnecessary worry because treating other people is simple.

So here is a simple approach that you can use: close your eyes, maybe put your hands in the prayer position, and take a few long deep breaths to calm you and still your mind. You should have in mind that the energy you will channel should be for the highest good of the recipient, but there is no particular form of words that you need to use when commencing your treatment. Now we are going to focus your attention on connecting to the energy. Imagine that energy is flooding down to you from above, flooding through your crown, through the centre of your body, down to your Dantien (an energy centre two fingerbreadths below your tummy button and 1/3rd of the way into your body). Imagine the energy building up and intensifying there. You are filling with energy. Now direct your attention towards the recipient and imagine that you are merging with them, becoming one with them. Feel compassion and enjoy the moment.

You may now begin your treatment, and maybe it would be nice to rest your hands on their shoulders for a while, to connect to them and to get the energy flowing. What hand positions you use will vary depending on what you were taught – there are many variations – and they are all variations on a theme, a way of firing the energy from lots of different directions to give it the best chance of getting to where it needs to go. Hand-positions for treating others are not set in stone and do not have to be followed slavishly. They are just there as a set of guidelines to follow to build your confidence when treating others, and with time and practice you will start to leave behind these basic instructions and gear any treatment towards the needs of the recipient on that occasion, perhaps based on what you picked up when you were 'scanning' and perhaps based on intuitive impressions, where you feel drawn to a particular area of the body. Don't try and work out 'why' you have felt drawn to a particular area of the body: just accept your impression and go with it.

Reiki is basically a hands-on treatment method, though for reasons of comfort and propriety you will choose to hover your hands over the recipient in some areas rather than resting on the body. I do not plaster my hands over the recipient's face or throat, for example, because I think that this is uncomfortable and unsettling for the person you are working on.

You do not have to hover your hands for every hand position, as some people are taught, and equally you do not have to keep at least one hand in physical contact with the recipient's body at all times, for fear of 'losing' your connection: your connection to the recipient is a state of mind, and where your hands are is irrelevant!

As you treat, you should aim to feel yourself merging with the energy, becoming one with the energy, to imagine yourself disappearing into the energy, and this can give you a quite blissful experience. Your mind may wander, particularly in the early stages of your Reiki practice, but you do not need to worry about this. If you notice thoughts intruding, pay them no attention; let them drift on like clouds. If you make a big effort to try and get rid of your thoughts then you will have in your head the original thoughts and then all the new thoughts about getting rid of the first lot of thoughts... you have made things worse! Just bring your attention gently back to the recipient, to the energy, feel yourself disappearing into the energy, merging with the recipient, and let the energy flow; your treatment can become a wonderful meditation.

It is not acceptable to chat to other people while giving a Reiki treatment. If you want to be an effective channel for the energy then you need to direct your attention to the work at hand and make sure you are not unduly distracted. For this reason, conversation between yourself and the recipient should be restricted. Reiki works best of you are still and focused, merging with the energy, in a gentle meditative state. Developing this state takes practice and you can't do it properly if you are chatting.

You do not need to stay for a particular set amount of time for each hand position. Though it would be probably be best to stay for a few minutes in each position, if in a particular hand position you feel a lot of energy coming through your hands then you can stay in that position for longer – sometimes a lot longer – until the sensation subsides and you can then move onto the next area. Your hands can guide you. Work from the head and shoulders, down the length of the body, and it is nice to finish with the ankles. Many people are taught to smooth down the energy field at the end of a session, and that is a nice thing to do, but remember that you do not have to follow any rituals slavishly, particularly in terms of any sort of 'closing' ritual; you do not need to touch the ground, you do not need to say a particular set of words, you do not need to visualise anything in particular, and you do not need to make any 'set' movements of your hands or body.

The Reiki Precepts

On your First Degree course you will have been introduced to the Reiki Precepts, or Reiki Principles, Mikao Usui's "rules to live by'". Just in case you have been given a slightly distorted version of the precepts, here is a more accurate translation:

> *The secret of inviting happiness through many blessings*
> *The spiritual medicine for all illness*
>
> *For today only: Do not anger; Do not worry*
> *Be humble*
> *Be honest in your dealings with people*
> *Be compassionate to yourself and others*
>
> *Do gassho every morning and evening*
>
> *Keep in your mind and recite*
>
> *The founder, Usui Mikao*

Any reference to 'honouring your elders, parents and teachers' is a later addition to the list, and is not what Mikao Usui taught.

The precepts were the hub of the whole system, and it is said that as much spiritual development can come through following the precepts in your daily life as would come from any energy work, so they are important. If we can try to focus on living in the moment, not forever dwelling on the past or worrying about the future (fear is a distraction), if we can remind ourselves of the many blessings we have in our lives, if we can forgive ourselves for not being perfect and if we can see things from another's point of view, if we can be compassionate towards ourselves as well as others, then we have gone a long way towards achieving a liberating sense of serenity and contentment. This is not something to be achieved overnight, of course: it is a work-in-progress.

Finally

Reiki has the potential to make an amazing, positive difference to you and the people around you. Remember that Reiki is simplicity itself, and by taking some steps to work on yourself regularly, and share Reiki with the people close to you, you are embarking on a very special journey.

How far you travel on that journey is governed by how many steps you take.

Notes

The Precepts

May 2004

Mikao Usui gave his students a series of 'precepts' to follow. The Concise Oxford Dictionary (9th Edition) defines a precept as (1) a command, a rule of conduct, and (2) a moral instruction, and they are an important part of Buddhist practice. We know that Mikao Usui was a Tendai Buddhist, and so precepts would have been an important part of his spiritual life. Lay followers of Buddhism generally undertake to follow (at least one of) five precepts, which are given in the form of promises to oneself: "I will (try) to...". Here are the five Buddhist precepts:

1. To refrain from harming living creatures (killing).
2. To refrain from taking that which is not freely given (stealing).
3. To refrain from sexual misconduct.
4. To refrain from incorrect speech (lying, harsh language, slander, idle chit-chat).
5. To refrain from intoxicants which lead to loss of mindfulness.

So precepts are a list of guidelines for living your life. They are not framed in terms of "thou shalt not..." as in the Judaeo-Christian tradition but rather are a set of ideals to work towards, recommendations about thought and behaviour that you should follow as much as you can.

Everyone who has learned Reiki will have, or should have, seen the Reiki precepts – Mikao Usui's 'rules to live by' – and they are available in a variety of different forms in different lineages. There is actually some difference between the precepts that Mikao Usui was teaching and the precepts that are quoted commonly in the West. For example, some Western versions of the precepts include an extra item: "honour your parents, elders and teachers". This is not original and seems to have been added by Mrs Takata to make the "list of rules to live by" more acceptable to her (largely) Christian American audience.

There has been some speculation about where Mikao Usui's precepts come from. It has been claimed that they originate in a book that was published in Usui's time, and it has been claimed that they are based on the edicts of Mutsuhito, the Meiji Emperor. Certainly it seems that many Tendai and Zen Buddhist teachers were passing on similar principles in Usui Sensei's time.

But now we know that Usui's precepts were his wording of an earlier set of precepts that have been traced back to the early 9th century, precepts that were used in a Tendai sect of Shugendo with which Usui Sensei was in contact. These precepts were a way of addressing aspects of the Buddhist eight-fold path in a simplified form, and they are the very 'hub' of the whole system. The precepts were the baseline, the foundation of Usui Sensei's teachings, and it was thought that individual could achieve as much spiritual development by following the precepts as could be achieved by carrying out all the energy exercises.

Incidentally, you may find some commentators saying that negative affirmations are not a good idea: such things are said to be more effective when framed in positive terms. What we have presented to us in the precepts is just a quirk of translation from Japanese to English: the precepts are actually a recommendation that we exist in the moment in a state where we are free from anger and worry, a 'worry-free, anger-free' state.

For me, Mikao Usui's precepts represent both some of the beneficial effects that Reiki can produce in your life if you work with the energy regularly, and they represent a set of principles that we need to follow to enhance our journey of self-healing and self-development with Reiki.

My main purpose in writing this article is to introduce you to a way of working with the precepts in conjunction with the Reiki energy. This is something that I have been experimenting with: a way of directly experiencing the effects of a precept in terms of energy flow.

I would like to suggest that you do the following, for a couple of minutes at a time, twice a day, for a month: Sit with your eyes closed and your hands resting in your lap, palms up. You are going to be releasing energy through your hands.

Stage One

Sit comfortably with your eyes closed and your hands resting in your lap, palms up. Take a few long deep breaths and feel yourself becoming peaceful and relaxed. Your mind empties. Say to yourself "I now release all my anger…"; say this three times to yourself if you like. Allow energy to be released through your palms, and be still until the flow of energy subsides. This may take a little while, particularly the first time you try this exercise.

Stage Two

Now say to yourself "I now release all my worry…"; say this three times to yourself if you like. Again allow a flurry of energy to leave your hands and be still until it subsides. Again this may take a little while, particularly the first time you try this exercise.

Alternatively, try carrying out the releasing exercise in time with your breath. Breathe in gently, say to yourself "I now release all my anger…" and then breathe out, allowing your anger to flood out of you on the out breath. Gently breath in, and repeat.

Notes

Mindfulness and Compassion

August 2003

In this article I want to talk about Mindfulness and Compassion, which I believe are two essential components of Reiki practice. Whether we are treating others, working on ourselves, empowering others or living our lives with Reiki, we should grow to embody those two states, the essence of the Reiki precepts.

Mindfulness

According to Usui Sensei's surviving students, Mikao Usui introduced his students to the practice of mindfulness at First Degree level, and emphasised this more at Second Degree level. According to the Concise Oxford Dictionary (9th Edition), to be mindful is to take heed or care, to be conscious. Mindfulness or being mindful is being aware of your present moment. You are not judging, reflecting or thinking. You are simply observing the moment in which you find yourself, fully aware. Moments are like a breath. Each breath is replaced by the next breath. You are there with no other purpose than being awake and aware of that moment.

So mindfulness is a state of living in the moment, of being relaxed, calm and fully engaged in what we are doing. Mindfulness is being fully aware of what is happening right now and giving ourselves completely to our task without distraction. By learning how to enjoy and be in the present moment we can find peace within ourselves.

Like precepts, mindfulness is largely associated with Buddhism and it is a meditative practice that is not reserved for special meditation sessions: it is a practice that you can embrace as part of your daily life and when carrying out routine and mundane tasks.

The best guide that I have found to the use of mindfulness as part of your daily life is the following book, written by Thich Nhat Hanh: "The Miracle of Mindfulness" and I recommend that all Reiki practitioners and teachers obtain a copy and practise being mindful during their daily activities.

I believe that Mikao Usui's precepts are all about mindfulness, and that when we are exhorted by the precepts to "just for today" release anger and worry, we are being guided to exist as far as we can in a mindful state. Anger and worry are distractions, you see, and if we can exist in the moment by being mindful then we will not dwell on the past and beat ourselves up for things that did not go the way we wanted, and we will not dwell on the future, perhaps worrying about things that have not yet happened. We can learn to release our attachments to the past and the future and just "be" now, content and accepting in the moment, by learning to be mindful.

Compassion

The final precept, that of being "compassionate towards ourselves and others" is for me an exhortation to be gentle with ourselves, to be patient, to be light-hearted, to not take ourselves quite so seriously and above all to be forgiving – first of all of ourselves but also of others. By accepting and forgiving ourselves we start to release our anger and our worry, and move towards a state of contentment in the moment.

The original system was a spiritual path, a path to enlightenment, and the precepts were what Usui Sensei's system was all about. These principles are a foundation for everything we do with Reiki: the states of mindfulness and compassion arise from following the precepts and from working with Reiki.

For example, how do we feel when we carry out a Reiki treatment? Treating someone with Reiki is a special, special gift. We feel a closeness, an intimacy, a merging with the recipient; we receive trust and we experience compassion. Ideally we should just be there in the moment, with the energy, with the recipient, with no expectations. We do not treat someone with the intention to resolve their health problem or eliminate their headache. We just merge with the energy and allow Reiki to do its work; we create a sacred space for healing to occur. If our mind wanders, as it may do, then we notice this and gently but firmly bring our attention back to the present and what we are doing. We become one with the energy as it flows through us, we become one with the recipient, and we experience that blissful contentment in the moment. When we treat we are mindful: we are an observer, not a participant.

Though some are taught that you can hold a conversation with someone as you treat, or watch television at the same time, this really will not lead to the best being given to the recipient. To be the most effective channel we can be, we need to be there with the energy, fully and gently engaged in our work, giving ourselves fully to the task without distraction.

Those same principles apply when working on ourselves, whether carrying out Hatsurei ho or self-treating. The state we should seek to achieve is that of being fully engaged in the endeavour, of being with the energy without distraction, merged, aware and simply existing in the moment, with a gentle feeling of forgiveness, love and compassion towards ourselves.

So both Mindfulness and Compassion are fundamental to our life with Reiki, fundamental to the Reiki precepts, to working on others and working on ourselves. Not surprisingly they are also an essential component of the transmission of Reiki to another person through carrying out Reiju empowerments. Reiju is the 'connection ritual' that Usui Sensei used, and taught to his surviving students. It is simple, elegant and powerful, free from the clutter and detail that surrounds most Western attunement styles. When we perform Reiju we have no expectations: we are there in the moment with the energy, following the prescribed movements. We are relaxed and fully engaged in what we are doing, aware of what is happening right now, and we give ourselves completely to our task without distraction. That is the essence of Reiju, the essence of treatments, the essence of the precepts, and the essence of our life with Reiki.

Notes

The Kaizen of Reiki

November 2002

If you have come across the word 'kaizen' before it will probably have been in the context of industrial quality control or personal development. "Kaizen" is a Japanese word that is usually translated as 'improvement', but it means more than that. The word has connotations of continuous, gradual, orderly and never-ending improvement, the willingness to constantly, relentlessly pursue improvement a small step at a time. The application of the kaizen principle is the reason why Japan's economy was transformed after the Second World War. All workers were encouraged to make suggestions as to how quality and production could be improved, even by tiny, tiny percentages, but over time the effect of these tiny percentage improvements, applied consistently and built upon, transformed Japanese industry.

So what has this to do with Reiki? Well the word kaizen actually appears towards the end of the Reiki precepts. The line in Japanese is "Shin shin kaizen, Usui Reiki Ryoho", which could be loosely translated as "Mind body change it for better Usui Reiki method". So when Usui was talking about using his system to improve the body and mind, I get the impression that we are looking at a lifelong commitment to work with the system, to focus the energy on ourselves again and again, long-term, in order to produce small incremental improvements within ourselves, to dedicate ourselves to developing our effectiveness as a channel. But small changes build on previous small changes, an enhancement upon an enhancement leads to amazing development over time. And Usui's original system gives us the solid, concrete techniques that we can use to develop ourselves: as channels, in terms of spirituality and in terms of intuition, to produce our own individual Reiki Evolution!

So how do we pursue our own kaizen of Reiki? How do we apply the concept of continuous and never-ending improvement to our practice of Reiki? Here are a few suggestions...

Root your practice of Reiki in daily energy work.

If you are serious about wanting to obtain the many benefits that are available to you through the Reiki system then you are going to have to work on yourself most days, ideally every day, and by doing so you will build up the beneficial effects of Reiki within you. It is not sufficient to use Reiki on yourself once a week, or to assume that if you treat other people occasionally then this is enough to give you the Reiki you need.

Your first priority should be yourself, and this means daily energy work. This does not need to be an onerous task, nor does it need to take a long time to carry out. Sometimes we decline to use Reiki on ourselves because we do not have the perfect opportunity, perhaps because we do not have, say, 30 minutes to work on ourselves. Yet even 10 minutes of energy work, when carried out consistently each day, would be far better and produce much better results than doing nothing for days, and then a great big blitz for a big chunk of time on a weekend to try and 'catch up'. Spending even a small chunk of time working on ourselves each day builds up a momentum and stirs changes which build and build. Sporadic practice leads to some beneficial changes, but you are not maximising your Reiki potential.

So, how can we work on ourselves? Well, a good place to start would be to practise Hatsurei ho, a series of energy exercises taught in the Usui Reiki Ryoho Gakkai (the 'Gakkai), an association set up after Usui's death by the Imperial Officers who had trained with him for a while. 'Hatsurei ho' means something like 'start up Reiki technique' and consists of a series of energy meditations/ visualisations that focus on your Tanden (Dantien in Chinese) and which are designed to be carried out every day. The effects of Hatsurei ho are to:

1. Clear and cleanse your energy system
2. Help to move your energy system more into a state of balance
3. Help to ground you
4. Help to build up your personal energy reserves
5. Allows you to grow spiritually
6. Develop your ability as a channel for Reiki
7. Help to develop your sensitivity to the flow of energy
8. Help to develop your intuitive side

The exercises take perhaps 12-15 minutes to carry out each day, and can be fitted into the busiest of schedules if the will is there. We can all make this time for our Reiki practice.

But we should also focus the energy more specifically on ourselves, on our own self-healing, by carrying out a self-treatment each day. Whether you carry out the Western 'hands-on' method of treating yourself, or use the self-treatment meditation that Usui Sensei taught, you should focus the energy on yourself on a regular basis to help bring things into balance for you on all levels, and to help you to release things that no longer serve you: mental states, emotions, physical things. The energy will deal with many aspects of your body/mind, many deeply-embedded imbalances, if we give the energy the opportunity to do its work on us, digging deep and chipping away at the 'baggage' that we carry, over time.

We prefer to use Usui Sensei's self-treatment meditation because it seems more intense and versatile, but all self-treatment approaches are valid. Usui's Sensei's system was all about spiritual development and self-healing, so Hatsurei Ho and self-treatment can lie at the very heart of your Reiki practice. You need to put yourself first, and the principle of kaizen means that by working on yourself consistently, great transformations are possible. You owe it to yourself to allow yourself to obtain the benefits that are available to you through Reiki.

Receive spiritual empowerments throughout your training and beyond.

Training with Usui was rather like martial arts training, where you were in ongoing contact with your teacher over an extended period of time. Part of your training involved receiving simple spiritual empowerments from Usui Sensei, repeatedly, at all levels. Each empowerment reinforced your connection to the source, cleared your channel for the energy, allowed you to develop spiritually and enhanced your intuitive potential. To echo this practice, Taggart sends out a distant Reiju empowerment every week, on a Monday, which can be 'tuned in to' by any Reiki person. You can find out about this, and what to do, by visiting this page of the Reiki Evolution web site:

www.reiki-evolution.co.uk/reijubroadcast.htm.

On each occasion that you receive Reiju you are given what you need, and as your needs change from one occasion to another, this simple spiritual 'blessing' helps you to develop. A one-off attunement or empowerment does of course give you something permanent, and when you learn Reiki for the first time the attunements or empowerments that you receive provide you with the ability to use Reiki permanently, but it does not stop there: by receiving empowerments on a regular basis you are building momentum and allowing the energy to penetrate more deeply within you.

If we are committed to ongoing improvements within ourselves then we should make the time to receive an empowerment weekly. And again it is the regular commitment which is the key, the key to deepening your experience of the energy and its beneficial effects on you.

Work on developing your intuitive potential.

Mikao Usui's original system did not focus very much on the treatment of others, and any instruction on treatments would not have involved slavishly following a set of 'standard' hand positions that you had to apply to everyone you treated. Usui's method was simpler and more elegant. You allowed the energy to guide your hands to the right place to treat, different from one person to another, and different within the same person from one treatment to another. The way we have been taught to do this is through a 'technique' called 'Reiji Ho' (indication of the spirit technique'), a way of emptying your mind and merging with the energy, getting your head out of the way to allow intuition to bubble to the surface. The exciting thing about Reiji Ho is that it works for everyone, and with time - we come back to kaizen's small incremental improvements - your hands will move more quickly, more consistently, more effortlessly, and you will start to attract more intuitive information. So every time we treat someone we should spend time cultivating our 'Reiji' state of mind, and gradually, gradually, we develop.

Learn to become the energies.

...that you are introduced to at Second Degree and Master levels. Usui's system didn't involve symbols as far as most of his students were concerned. Students were expected to carry out meditations over an extended period of time in order to learn to experience different energies and, at Second Degree, students were introduced to the energies of "earth ki" and "heavenly ki", which represent two fundamental aspects of our being. By practising 'becoming' earth ki and heavenly ki again and again – a powerful self-healing practice - these energies became so familiar to the students that they could 'connect' to the energy direct without having to use a prop like a symbol. Usui provided some Shinto mantras for some of his students to use to invoke the energies, but it was possible to move beyond these mantras with time, too. In my article 'A Simple Way with Symbols' I describe a meditation that you can use to 'become' these energies.

But again we see that to obtain the greatest benefit, to enhance self-healing, to free up our practice and move beyond symbols, takes time and commitment. A quick meditation carried out a few times is not enough: Usui Sensei's students spent 6-9 months meditating on just one energy, and this was done because the principle of kaizen – plugging away and developing by small amounts again and again – led to deep changes over time.

Live your life according to Usui's guiding principles.

Usui's simple principles to live by offer perhaps the best example of the principle of kaizen in our Reiki practice: Usui Sensei's precepts are a work in progress. They are not something that you read through and think "OK, got that": the precepts are simple to read and understand but they are something that you drip-feed into your daily life over time, more and more over time.

We may begin by thinking about the precepts when we first come across them on a First Degree course: we reflect on how they might impinge on our lives, our thoughts and emotions, our behaviour; we might imagine situations from that past that might have proceeded better had we exemplified the precepts, and we might imagine situations in the future and see ourselves behaving in a way that demonstrates that we are living the precepts.

But this initial surge of interest in the precepts is not sufficient to produce the beneficial changes that the precepts can produce in our lives.

To fully embrace Usui Sensei's spiritual principles takes regular reflection and ongoing thought. On an ongoing basis we consider our thoughts and our behaviour, we reflect on the principles and what they mean to us. If we do this then over time we will find that living the precepts becomes easier, that our behaviour is modifying itself, that there are more permanent changes in the way that we react and behave and relate to other people. But this will only happen if we 'chip away' at our current behaviour patterns, using the precepts as our guiding light. There are no quick fixes: the precepts are not just for First Degree. The precepts are the essence of our Reiki practice.

Now, we do not need to be perfect, we do not need to beat ourselves up for not applying each and every principle on all occasions, but by dedicating ourselves, and by forgiving ourselves, and by trying to do a little better each day than we did the day before, we transform ourselves.

That is the key to our kaizen of Reiki: dedication and commitment, patience and forgiveness, and openness to the source. Long term.

Notes

Get out of the way!

November 2005

In this short article I want to talk about the best way to approach working on other people, whether giving treatments or carrying out distant healing. I want to talk about our state of mind and our intent when channelling the energy.

The first thing I want to say is that we are just a channel for the energy, not the source of the energy. This seems an obvious thing to say, but we need to remember that we are not healers. We do not heal. We do not have that power. What we do when we treat someone is simply to create a 'healing space' that the recipient can use to move more into a state of balance. The recipient is responsible for their own healing, for what they experience or don't experience; they are responsible for how they react to the treatment. They are healing themselves. We are just necessary bystanders in the process: we do not direct the energy and we do not determine the outcome.

So I am not so happy with the title "Reiki Healer" because it suggests that the Reiki practitioner has the power to heal; they do not. I don't think that the title "Reiki Necessary Bystander" is going to catch on, so I prefer to use the title "Reiki Practitioner". It describes what we do: we practise Reiki and it does not imply that we have the power to heal others.

This article is called "Get out of the way" because I believe that this is the best thing we can do when treating someone or when sending distant healing. We are not the source of the healing; we are not the source of the energy, so we do not need to be there, directing and controlling. We can stand aside and if we do so then the energy can flow strongly and clearly, without interference from us.

When we treat someone we are not 'cheerleading' for a particular end result: we do not give Reiki to get rid of someone's head ache, or back ache, or to resolve their Gall

Bladder problem, though of course these things may result from channelling Reiki. End results are out of our hands and to focus strongly on a particular purpose for the treatment is not helpful. Reiki will not be controlled by us in terms of end results and attempts to control the energy in this way just puts up barriers that prevent the energy from doing what it needs to do. Rather like the well-meaning amateur who gets in the way and prevents the professional from doing their job properly, our attempts to focus the energy to produce a particular end result will hinder the process for the recipient.

So our intent when treating someone or sending distant healing is that the energy should do whatever is appropriate for the recipient. We are neutral, we are detached, and we do not focus on outcomes. Ideally we should drift into a gentle meditative state when treating or sending distant healing, and this can be best achieved by our 'disappearing' into the energy, feeling ourselves merging with or becoming one with the energy. We merge with the energy and we merge with the recipient; we are empty. We do by not doing.

Though some people are taught that it is ok to talk and chat to people, or bystanders, when giving a Reiki treatment, to do such a thing is neither professional nor does it lead to effective treatments. If we are distracted then the energy flows less strongly, so if we want to do the best for our clients then we need to keep quiet, and encourage the client to keep quiet too. You can try an experiment for yourself if you like, to prove to yourself that distraction lessens the strength of your Reiki. You could try this at a Reiki share, for example. Start by resting your hands on someone's shoulders and allow the energy to flow for a while. Then deliberately start up a conversation with someone sitting near you: take your attention away from the recipient and fully engage in the conversation. Do this for a few minutes. Then bring your attention back to the recipient, be still and quiet, and allow the energy to flow. How has the recipient's experience of the energy varied?

Now, we do not need to be in a perfect meditative state in order to be an effective channel for Reiki, but it certainly helps to cultivate a still and empty mind. We are all human and it is perfectly normal for unwanted thoughts to appear in our head. But we should pay them no attention. If we pay the unwanted thoughts attention and try to get rid of them we then have two lots of thoughts: the thoughts we did not want and all the new thoughts about the need to get rid of the first lot of thoughts. We have made things worse!

The best approach to unwanted thoughts, then, is to allow them to drift by like clouds: pay them no attention, do not engage with them. They will leave. Some more may come, but pay them no attention either. In time you should find that your busy mind starts to quieten and some of your treatments will become beautiful meditations, with your mind emptying with the energy, and staying empty. Some treatments will not be like this, of course, but we do not need to be perfect. We can cultivate a more meditative state over time, moving in the right direction, and without worrying too much about individual occasions when our untamed brain kept on talking to us. This is a work-in-progress!

So Reiki is simple: you empty your head, you merge with the energy, do you not direct, you do not control, you do not try; you empty yourself and merge with the recipient, standing aside to allow the energy do what it needs to do, without interference from us.

Notes

Reiki Sensations

February 2006

In this article I would like to talk about the sort of things that students might feel – or not feel – when receiving attunements or empowerments, when working with energy and when treating or being treated, and the significance of these sensations. The article is particular addressed to people who have just taken a First Degree course or who are only just starting on their journey with Reiki, though it should be of interest to people at all Reiki levels.

Attunements or empowerments

(Please note that, to avoid unnecessary repetition, I am going to use the word 'empowerment' to refer both to Reiju empowerments and Western-style Reiki attunements.)

When we arrive on a Reiki First Degree course, we probably have very little idea of what we might experience when going through an empowerment. If you read books about Reiki, everyone seems to be going through an exceptional, once-in-a-lifetime experience, but for most people it really isn't like that.

There is no way of predicting what an individual will experience when receiving an empowerment, whether in person or at a distance. You may have an amazing experience, or you may feel very little or nothing. It is not uncommon for people to see some colours or feel some heat or tingling or pulsing or pressure in various areas of their bodies. For some people an empowerment is a unique experience, profound, emotional, an experience that is almost unbelievable. For others very little happens.

Sometimes you might find that there will be four people, say, on a course. Three people are talking about the surprising, or interesting, or special experiences that they just had, and one poor soul is sitting there thinking to themselves "I knew this wouldn't work for me… I know Reiki is supposed to work for everyone, but it hasn't worked for me". We assume that if we notice a lot happening then the empowerment has 'taken', that it has worked really well, and we assume that if we felt very little – or if we felt nothing – then the connection ritual has not worked, that we haven't been attuned, or we haven't been attuned properly.

But what a student experiences when they receive an empowerment is no guide as to the effectiveness of that empowerment. In fact what a student experiences really is irrelevant, because empowerments always work. Of course it is nice and reassuring to have the "bells and whistles and fireworks" – it helps you to believe that something definite has happened - but someone who has noticed all these things has not been more effectively empowered when compared with a student who felt very little or nothing.

Experiences are interesting, but not important. They don't mean anything in terms of whether, or how well, an empowerment has worked, because empowerments always work, no matter what the student feels or doesn't feel.

Experiencing energy

People are all different, and people differ in terms of how sensitive they are to the flow of energy in the early stages of their work with Reiki. Sometimes people arrive on a Reiki course massively sensitive to the energy, and perhaps better able to sense subtle differences than is their teacher, and that's nice for them, while other people may notice something very subtle, or perhaps nothing at all. Most people will feel something.

So when playing with energy, most people will feel something in between their hands when they try to make an energy ball. Most people will feel something when they try to feel someone else's energy field, or if they practise 'scanning' (assuming that there is something there to detect – there won't always be). But not everyone will feel these things to begin with, and the people who do not feel anything should not be disheartened: because sensitivity to such things can develop with practice and repetition. Most people will find that, no matter how sensitive they find themselves when they first learn Reiki, when they start to work with the energy regularly – for example by carrying out Hatsurei ho every day, and by self-treating – their sensitivity to the energy will increase. But this is a work-in-progress and we may need to be patient. And we may find that our sensitivity to the energy never reaches our goal, or is never as great as other Reiki people that we come across. Maybe we are setting an unreasonable target for ourselves.

And we should remember that sensitivity to the flow of energy is not the be-all and end-all of Reiki. We can work on ourselves and derive the many benefits that come through Reiki, no matter what we feel or don't feel when we carry out hatsurei ho or self-treat. We can treat other people effectively no matter what we might feel or not feel in our hands. I have come across several successful and effective Reiki Master / Teachers who do not feel anything going on in their hands, and never have done. The reason why they continued their Reiki training, rather than giving up in the face of no physical sensations to encourage them, was because they practised on lots of people and they could see, by the positive responses they received from the recipients, that something was definitely going on, that they were doing good things, that Reiki was certainly doing something for the people they treated even though they couldn't feel the energy.

You may ask how you can treat someone when you can't feel anything, or if you can't scan very well at the moment. Well, most people in the world of Reiki are taught a standard set of hand positions to use when they treat, and these standard positions can be followed, giving general coverage over the body; the energy is drawn to areas of need, so that works perfectly well. Not everyone scans. Not everyone is taught how to scan. It isn't a vital step in a treatment, but it can be a useful one to perform if you can do it.

But if you can work intuitively then of course you can place your hands in the right places for each person you work on, and stay in each position for the most appropriate amount of time, not based on the sensations you are feeling in your hands but based on your intuitive impressions. Everyone can work intuitively with some practice, and you may well be taught how to carry out "Reiji ho" (a Japanese method for opening to your intuition during a treatment) on a Second Degree course. So an intuitive approach to treatments actually eliminates any advantage in being able to sense strongly in your hands.

Sensations experienced by people you treat

Now, you will not be surprised to know that the experiences of people being treated also varies a great deal. For some people, on some occasions, treatments are very strong. They might feel intense heat from the practitioner's hands, see coloured lights, drift in and out of consciousness. And on other occasions that same person might feel the treatment to be mild and gentle. The energy is drawn by the recipient in amounts that are appropriate for them on that occasion, so the perceived 'strength' of any treatment is determined by the recipient's need. The practitioner is just a necessary bystander in the treatment process.

While some people seem to quite often notice a lot happening when they are treated, there are also people who feel very little or nothing when they receive a Reiki treatment, no matter who they receive the treatment from. If you have just started out on your Reiki journey and you just happen to treat one of these people, or a few of these people, as your first 'clients' then you may end up disheartened, thinking that their lack of a strong sensation means that you are ineffective as a practitioner. We want the recipient to feel a lot because that reassures us that we are doing things 'correctly', that we are effective as a channel for the energy. But things aren't always so simple: while quite often there may be general correlation between what the practitioner feels and what the recipient feels (a very hot area for the practitioner is felt as a very tingly area, say, for the recipient) this correlation will not always be there and, sometimes, you might find a practitioner feeling a raging furnace in their hands, amazed at the strength of what is going on, while the recipient did not notice anything at all, and perhaps didn't notice anything at all during the entire treatment!

Summary

So really this whole article boils down to one simple phrase: "just for today, do not worry". While it is perfectly natural to want to have some physical sensations to help us believe that we are really doing something when we use Reiki on ourselves and on other people, and while most people who learn Reiki will receive sufficient feedback to reassure them, this will not always happen. With practice and experience we start to let go of the need to be reassured by what we and others feel, and we come to realise that no matter what we feel or don't feel, Reiki is working for us. But it can be difficult to accept this in the early stages, particularly if we are a little sceptical.

If you aren't feeling too much at the moment my advice to you is to follow the instructions you were given: carry out your Hatsurei ho every day, self-treat regularly, and get your hands on as many people as you can. Do short blasts on someone's knee or shoulder, treat people in a straight-backed chair for 20-30 minutes, do full treatments; go with the time you have you have available. The important thing is to get the hands-on practice and you will find, if you treat a good cross-section of people, that you will receive from them the positive feedback that you need, and with sufficient practice you may find that you start to notice more with time.

So be patient, don't worry, and have fun with your Reiki.

Notes

Restrictions on Reiki

November 2001

Depending on whom you trained with, you may have been given quite a long list of 'situations where you should not use Reiki'. It seems that the only restriction that Mrs Takata taught was that you should not treat a broken bone with Reiki, but many other restrictions have been added in later on in Reiki's Western history. I thought I would spend a little time talking about these 'Reiki contraindications'.

Firstly, I would like to talk about the 'broken bone' restriction. This is made on the basis that Reiki accelerates the healing process, so you do not want Reiki to set the bone before it has been put back in the right position. Now while Reiki is an amazing energy, and has done some wonderful and breathtaking things, I think most people's experience is that Reiki gently supports the body's natural healing ability, and that while it may accelerate the healing process, the effects of Reiki generally build up cumulatively. I do not believe that Reiki will set someone's bone like fast-acting Polyfilla, so that they will have to have the bone re-broken and re-set when they get to Casualty a few hours later. Breaking a bone is a shocking and painful experience (I know this from first hand experience!) and Reiki could make a real difference to someone, so I would not hold back from giving it, and I would not hold back from treating the area where the bone is broken. Suggesting that you could Reiki someone, but keep well away from the broken bone, does not stop Reiki from rushing to where it is needed (the bone), and why would we imagine that what many people see as a spiritually-guided life-force energy would mess things up for a person. Reiki is supposed to be intelligent.

Another situation where some people are taught that you 'should not treat' is when a client has a pacemaker. This restriction is made on the basis that Reiki energy is electromagnetic in nature, and will interfere with the proper functioning of the device. Confusingly, some say that this restriction only applies to analogue pacemakers, not the newer digital ones. There seems to be no evidence whatsoever to indicate that Reiki would cause a problem in this area, and I have not heard on a single anecdote where a Reiki practitioner treated someone with a pacemaker and the treatment caused problems. I am also not aware of any evidence to show that Reiki is electromagnetic in nature, either. If it was, you could measure Reiki easily: move your hand over a wire and you would induce an electric current, which you could pick up with a voltmeter. Some have suggested that you can solve this 'problem' by keeping away from the heart area, but we all know that Reiki rushes from where we put it to where it is needed. I would have thought that a person with a pacemaker needed more Reiki in the heart area, not less, and if Reiki is drawn to the areas of need then it is going to go where it wants anyway. The only solution would be not to treat someone with a pacemaker, which I think is ridiculous. Some have suggested that you should not attune someone with a pacemaker, and again I do not think that this is sensible. I am not going to restrict my practice of Reiki on the basis of unfounded supposition.

With nearly all the restrictions that are put on Reiki, there seems to be no evidence to back up any of them. I am not talking about double blind clinical trials here, but even simple anecdotes where a practitioner has treated someone and found that there is a problem that can be reasonably attributed to the treatment that has been given. I have heard that you should not treat insulin-dependent Diabetics, or people taking steroids for adrenal insufficiency. Those restrictions have been made on the basis that if Reiki produces an instant cure then the patient's next dose of insulin, or steroids, will kill them. Again, while Reiki is a wonderful healing force, it is not my belief that Reiki is likely to cure diabetes, for example, at the click of a finger. Most people's experience is that the effects of Reiki build up cumulatively and that if a condition has taken a long time to develop, then it is not so likely to disappear straight away. Yes, a diabetic patient's blood glucose levels may vary after a Reiki treatment, but diabetics' blood sugar levels vary a great deal anyway. That is why they have to keep on sticking themselves with a pin to monitor their levels, and you could only attribute this variation to Reiki if it happened consistently after treatments and their blood sugar levels were stable the rest of the time.

Having said that, there does seem to be some anecdotal evidence that Reiki treatments can sometimes cause the client's blood sugar levels to alter after a treatment. This does not mean that you should not treat diabetics: it means that you need to keep this in mind and mention this possibility to the client, so that they can monitor their blood sugar levels accordingly.

I have heard that you should not send distant Reiki to someone who is driving a car, because they will fall asleep, and you should not send distant Reiki to someone who is under an anaesthetic, because it will make them wake up... well, which is it? This doesn't sound like an intelligent energy to me, and there seems to be a lot of fear, and a lack of trust in the energy, underlying all these restrictions. So where is the evidence that Reiki wakes people up during surgery? Where is even one anecdote where it was clear that Reiki, rather than any other cause, led to this happening? Look for the evidence, and you find that these scare stories have no foundation.

In fact, the restrictions do not stop there. There are many more taught in different lineages. For example, you should not treat people with cancer, you should not treat people who are pregnant, you should not treat people who are depressed or who have asthma, you should not treat people who are stressed, you should not treat young children, you should not treat animals, you should not treat people who are taking homoeopathic remedies, you should not treat people who are taking medicines, you should not treat people wearing green trousers (sorry, I made that one up!).

Let's just examine two of these. It is said by some teachers that you should not treat people who have cancer because Reiki will "feed the cancer"; there is a variation on this myth, actually, where people are taught that they should not use one of the Reiki symbols because it will "put energy into the cancer". Let's think rationally about this for just a second: we have cancer cells inside us all of the time and as you sit reading this, there are cancer cells in you. Your cells go haywire all the time and your immune system detects the errors and kills the cells. But if you adhere to this Reiki contraindication then you should not treat anyone at all because Reiki feeds cancer cells, and everyone has cancer cells in them, so we can't treat people, or animals, we can't treat ourselves, and being attuned would be a death sentence!

And if we can't treat pregnant women then we really need to refrain from treating any women of childbearing age because of course women can be in the early stages of pregnancy and not know about it, or be pregnant and not know about it. And then of course all women of childbearing age should refrain from self-treating, and should not go on Reiki courses.

People do not think things through.

I believe that Reiki is a beautiful healing energy that supports the body's natural healing ability, and brings things into balance on all levels. It either has an innate intelligence, and knows where to go to an extent, or it is the body that is intelligent and draws the energy to where it is needed. In either case, Reiki is not going to mess up a person and leave them less well off than they were before they started, other than a temporary intensification of symptoms. Examples of these would be an emotional release or strong emotions felt for a few days after being treated, or joint pains getting worse during a treatment and then improving subsequently.

The last set of restrictions that I have heard about concern distant healing, where it is said in some quarters that you should not send Reiki to people who have not asked for or given their permission. Some people say that it is totally unethical to send distant Reiki to someone without obtaining their agreement and that it a gross intrusion. I do not agree with this, for a number of reasons:

1. Firstly, I see sending distant Reiki as rather like sending concentrated prayer. When you pray for someone you are asking for Divine intervention in another person's life, in whatever way is right for that person according to Divine will. You are asking for things to change for the better. When you send Reiki you are sending it with loving intent and for the person's highest good, so it is in line with that person's destiny or karma, and many people see Reiki energy as having Divine origins. You do not ring someone up to ask their permission to pray for them, so why should if be different with Reiki?
2. If someone were knocked over by a car a few yards away from you, would you really not send Reiki to them because you couldn't drag them into the seated position to sign a consent form? No. You would send Reiki to their highest good and let the energy do what is appropriate for them. You offer the energy: you do not force the recipient to receive it.
3. Reiki is a beautiful healing energy that brings things into balance on all levels and does not mess people up, leaving them worse off than they were to begin with. With distant healing your intent is that the energy works for the highest good of the recipient, so if it is not appropriate for that person to get the benefit of the energy then it simply will not work. You are not imposing your will and you are not imposing your preferred solution on the situation. You are simply sending love, offering the energy, making the energy available, not forcing it to be received.

For these reasons, I have no problem in sending Reiki to people who have not specifically requested it. I send the energy with the intention that it be received by the recipient at whatever time is appropriate for them. I do not see that there are any other restrictions that need to be applied to the energy, or the practice of Reiki. In the West we think too much, and come up with too many complications. Reiki is simple and does not need to be restricted. It knows what to do.

Notes

Intelligent Energy?

February 2001

It is well established within Reiki that the energy we channel is 'intelligent'. Some people believe that the energy is innately intelligent, perhaps because of its divine origins, and some believe that the intelligence of the energy is accounted for by the presence of spirit guides who direct the energy as we treat someone. Others believe that it is the body that is intelligent, drawing the energy to where it needs to go. Most of us will have noticed that the energy will move from where our hands are resting to other parts of the recipient's body, drawn according to the recipient's need to areas of need, so it is clear that it doesn't always restrict itself to where we place it.

Some people take the line that Reiki will work perfectly well no matter what hand positions you use, irrespective of the knowledge and experience of the practitioner and whether or not the practitioner can work intuitively. The implication of this is that you could quite happily carry out a Reiki treatment by simply holding someone's hands for an hour and the energy would be drawn to the areas of need, and that there is nothing that you could do to help make the treatment more effective.

Another view is that there are things that a practitioner can do in order to increase the effectiveness of a treatment, for example:

- Working on yourself to develop your ability as a channel
- Using intuition to decide where to put your hands (rather than following standard hand positions) and what aspect of the energy to emphasise during the treatment, or where to direct your attention.

There are some inconsistencies in the first view described above. Many people will use techniques designed to balance the chakras, while at the same time maintaining that Reiki is intelligent and will always give the recipient what they need. Yet imposing your will on the energy and using it to balance the chakras is over-riding the way that the energy will work in the body, is it not? Surely if Reiki is an intelligent energy then it will balance the recipient's chakras in a way that is appropriate for the individual, without the practitioner doing anything specific to achieve this. If you routinely direct Reiki to balance a person's chakras you are suggesting that Reiki will not balance the chakras without direct intervention by the practitioner. Since most people would agree that Reiki works on your energy system and produces beneficial effects on all levels, how could it not balance your chakras during this process?

Either Reiki is intelligent, in which case you don't need to spend time balancing people's chakras, or it isn't intelligent, in which case we would always need to move in to balance the chakras. But if Reiki can't even balance your chakras on its own, what on earth is it doing?

I believe that spending time balancing people's chakras using Reiki is unnecessary, and that Reiki will do to a person's chakras what needs to be done to achieve balance for them at the end of a treatment. Of course subsequently the chakras will drift out of balance again, back to their more habitual state, but I believe that by repeating a treatment you are showing the chakras what it is like to be in a state of balance, and that repeated exposure to this balanced state, by providing a series of treatments, helps to move the recipient's chakras more into a state of balance long-term.

Another challenge to the 'Reiki is perfectly intelligent, we do not need to develop ourselves as a channel, we do not need to work intuitively" point of view is the fact that people are able to develop an intuitive ability and find that their hands are guided into combinations of hand positions that are different from one person to another, and different from one treatment to another. This suggests, of course, that there are sequences of hand positions that are more appropriate or effective in dealing with an individual's problems on that occasion than simply applying a standard template. If a standard template is always sufficient – or just holding someone's hands for an hour is all that is needed – why would our hands be guided by the energy to direct the energy into particular areas, distinctive for that recipient and different from the hand positions elicited for another person?

In practice, I have found that people treated with intuitively-guided hand positions find that the energy seems to penetrate more deeply, that the treatments feel in some way more relevant, more profound, more effective than when standard positions are used, and that is my impression too. Treatments based on intuitively-guided hand positions seem more powerful, sometimes a lot more powerful, than treatments based on standard hand positions, since we are directing the energy into just the right combination, and sequence, of positions for that person on that occasion.

If we look to the origins of Reiki and the way that Mikao Usui taught, we can see that intuitive working was a fundamental part of the practice of Reiki, and still is in Mikao Usui's Reiki Association in Japan to this day. Why would Usui have placed so much emphasis on using intuition if standard hand positions - or no hand positions - are just as good in terms of producing good results? He was a practical man, after all. So there is something special about working intuitively: it seems to do more than standard hand positions can.

For the benefit of students who could not yet work intuitively (and that is the important point), Chujiro Hayashi produced a long list of what could be described as 'good places to put your hands for different medical conditions', which suggests that certain combinations of hand positions are more effective in dealing with specific conditions that applying a standard template. Why would Dr Hayashi have produced such a list if, as many believe, Reiki is an intelligent energy that always goes where it is needed? We should remember, though, that this list was a stopgap, and that intuitive working was the ideal.

The above suggests that although Reiki may be intelligent to an extent – or the recipient's body is intelligent to an extent – we can enhance our treatments through some of the things that we can do, for example allowing the energy to guide us in terms of where we place our hands.

Further inconsistencies in the 'Reiki is perfectly intelligent' point of view come through the use of symbols: if we think about it, as soon as we start using any of the Reiki symbols in the Western fashion, perhaps routinely drawing the symbols as we treat, in a pre-determined sequence, we are consciously over-riding the way that the energy wants to work when left to its own devices, and imposing our will by directing the energy in a certain way. Yet if the energy knows exactly what to and where to go, why would we need to use symbols? Why would we need to impose our control over the energy in this way?

But this is not the only way that the symbols can be used. Just in the same way that we can move beyond standard hand positions to embrace intuitive working, with all the benefits that are associated with this, we can also work intuitively when we use the symbols, allowing the energy to guide us in terms of which aspect of the energy we emphasise, if any, during a treatment. Thus we work in partnership with the energy.

I believe that Reiki is an intelligent energy to an extent, and is drawn by the recipient's need to the appropriate areas, sometimes over-riding the way that we have directed the energy if that is required. However, we can assist in providing just what the recipient needs on each occasion by working intuitively, by being open and allowing the energy to guide us. I believe that we work in partnership with the energy, and that we are not simply empty tubes through which the energy flows. Through the development of our intuition, we can understand how the energy needs to be directed by us to better help our clients: where best to put our hands, and what aspects of the energy need to be emphasised.

Notes

Notes

Developing your Reiki

This section begins with a summary of the basic practices and principles of Reiki Second Degree.

Next we examine some important aspects of the practice of Reiki, perhaps more applicable to Second Degree and above, but not exclusively so; for example, we consider two important energies introduced to the student at Second Degree, and we explore the potential of our intuition and the power of intent, two drivers of what we do when we practise Reiki, showing some of the things that are possible.

Finally, we focus on different aspects of simplicity when applied to the practice of Reiki, in general and in terms of the use of symbols.

Here are the articles, together with the dates when the original versions of the articles were published in the Reiki Evolution eZine.

Aug 2005	Back to Basics: Reiki Second Degree
May 2005	The Breath of Earth and Heaven
Feb 2002	Working with Intuition
Nov 2002	The Importance of Intent
Aug 2003	Remote Treatments
Aug 2000	Symbols, Attunements and Beyond
Aug 2002	Simplicity and Sandwiches
Feb 2003	A Simple Way with Symbols
Nov 2003	Feng Shui your Reiki

Back to Basics: Reiki Second Degree

August 2005

People learn Reiki for many reasons and come from an amazing variety of backgrounds, all attending for their own personal reasons. Reiki courses in the UK present a whole variety of approaches, some "traditional" Western-style, some more Japanese in content, some wildly different and almost unrecognisable, some free and intuitive, others dogmatic and based on rules about what you should always do and not do. Reiki is taught in so many ways, and students will tend to imagine that the way that they were taught is the way that Reiki is taught and practised by most other Reiki people.

What I have tried to do in this article is to present a simple guide to what in my view is the essence of Second Degree: what it's all about and what we should be doing and thinking about to get the most out of our experience of Reiki at this level. My words are addressed to anyone at Second Degree level, or anyone who would like to review the essence of Second Degree.

The first thing I want to say is that there should usually be an interval of a couple of months or so between First and Second Degree if you want to get the most out of your Reiki experience, and that it is unwise to take both Degrees back-to-back over a weekend. We would not take an advanced driving test the day after passing our basic driving test, so why would we believe that moving on to a more 'advanced' level with Reiki would be an effective way to learn when we have had no opportunity to get the hang of the basics of First Degree? Can we get the most out of Second Degree when we have had no opportunity to get used to working with and sensing and experiencing energy, when we have had no opportunity to enhance our effectiveness as a channel and our sensitivity to Reiki through regular practice, when we have had no opportunity to become familiar with a standard treatment routine and have had no opportunity to feel comfortable and confident in treating other people? Reiki is not a race, and we need to be familiar with the basics before moving on.

Second Degree is all about:

1. reinforcing or enhancing your connection to the energy
2. learning some symbols which you can use routinely when working on yourself or treating others
3. enhancing your self-healing
4. learning how to effect a strong distant connection (distant healing)

And ideally it is also about opening yourself up to your intuitive side so that you throw away the basic Reiki 'rule book' and go freestyle, gearing any treatments towards the individual needs of the recipient.

There are many approaches to doing these things, and I wanted below to touch on each one and to dispel some myths that may have been passed on.

Enhancing your Connection to the energy

On your Second Degree course you will have received some attunements or some empowerments. Attunements are not standard rituals within the world of Reiki and take many forms, some simpler and some more complex. They have evolved and changed greatly during their journey from teacher to teacher in the West. There is no "right way" to carry out an attunement and the individual details of a ritual do not matter a great deal. They all work. Equally, there is no "correct" number of attunements that have to be carried out at Second Degree level. Whether you receive one, two, or three attunements on your course, that is fine.

On your course you may have received some "empowerments" rather than attunements, though these are less common. The word "empowerment", or "Reiju empowerment", refers to a connection ritual that has come to us from some Japanese sources, and is closer in essence to the empowerment that Mikao Usui conveyed to his students. If you are receiving empowerments rather than attunements then you really need to have received three of them at least.

What we experience when receiving an attunement or an empowerment will vary a lot. Some people have fireworks and bells and whistles and that's nice for them; other people notice a lot less, or very little, or even nothing, and that's fine too. What we feel when we have an attunement is not a guide to how well it has worked for us. Attunements work, and sometimes we will have a strong experience, but it's not compulsory! Whether we have noticed a lot, or very little, the attunement will have given us what we need.

Since in Mikao Usui's system you would have received empowerments from him again and again, it would be nice if you could echo this practice by receiving further empowerments (or attunements) and perhaps these might be available at your teacher's Reiki shares or get-togethers, if they hold them. But it is possible to receive distant Reiju empowerments and various teachers make them freely available as a regular 'broadcast'. This is not essential, and your connection to Reiki once given does not fizzle out, but it would be a beneficial practice if you could receive regular empowerments from someone.

Being "attuned" to a symbol

For many years within the world of Reiki, people believed that the symbols would not work for you, that they were essentially useless, until you had been "attuned" to the symbol: then it would work for you. Unfortunately the only connection rituals available in the West were 'attunements' which involved attuning you to a symbol, so no-one knew how to carry out a 'symbol-free' attunement to see if you really needed to be attuned to a symbol for it to work for you.

But in 1999, from Japan, emerged Reiju empowerments, a representation of the empowerments that Usui conferred, and these empowerments do not use symbols. Finally we were able to see if you really needed to be attuned to a symbol for it to work for you. Lo and behold we discovered that the symbols work fine for people who are connected to the energy using Reiju; they work fine for people who are connected to Reiki but who have not been 'attuned' to the symbols. It seems that once you are connected to Reiki – and now we know how to achieve this without symbols entering into the process – the symbols will work for you, and in fact any symbol seems to push the energy in a particular direction without you having to be specifically 'attuned' to it (whatever that means). The Reiki symbols are simply graphical representations of different aspects of the energy, a way of representing and emphasising what is already there.

"Sacred Symbols"

In some lineages students are not allowed to keep copies of the symbols and have to reproduce them from memory, based on what they learned on their Second Degree course. There is the suggestion that the symbols are sacred and not only sacred but secret, and should not be shown to people who are not involved in Reiki, or people who are at First Degree level. Where this idea came from in the Western Reiki system is not clear, since certainly Dr Hayashi had his students copy out his notes by way of preparing their own manuals, including copying down the symbols.

For me, the Reiki symbols are simply graphical representations of different aspects of the energy, useful tools to assist us in experiencing or becoming consciously aware of different aspects of what we already have, and what is special or sacred is our connection to the source, not the squiggles we might put on a piece of paper.

Because of the 'Chinese whispers' that have resulted from students not being allowed to take home hard copies of the Reiki symbols, there are many different versions of the symbols in existence, but they are mainly variations on a theme and they all seem to work in practice. Do remember, though, that the original CKR had an anticlockwise spiral, and to use a version of CKR with a clockwise spiral is to use a symbol that is not part of the Usui/Hayashi/Takata system.

Using Symbols in practice

Some students are taught there is one 'correct' way that symbols have to be used. Reiki is not so finicky. The important thing when using a Reiki symbol is to focus your attention on the symbol in some way, so whether you are drawing the symbol with your fingers hovering over the back of your hand as you treat someone, whether you are drawing out the symbol using eye movements, or nose movements, or in your mind's eye, all approaches will work. You do not need to visualise the symbols in a particular colour and if you can see the symbol in your mind's eye in its entirety – this takes practice - you can 'flash' the whole symbol rather than drawing it out stroke by stroke.

Just because we have been taught some symbols does not mean that we are now obliged to use them all the time when we treat or when we work on ourselves. They can be used to emphasise different aspects of the energy, but this is optional. Use of symbols does seem to boost the flow of energy, so we can use them when it feels appropriate. This is the key: to bring a symbol into a particular part of a treatment when we have a strong feeling that we ought to, to work intuitively rather than following a set method.

I have written in other articles below about the issue of simplicity within Reiki practice, and the complicated way that people have ended up using the Reiki symbols, for example mixing symbols together or using complicated symbol sandwiches. Remember that the simple approach is usually the most effective, and that there is no hard and fast way that you 'have' to work with the symbols you have been shown.

By the way, if you have been taught that you have to draw the three Second Degree symbols over your palm each day or else they will stop working for you, you can safely ignore these instructions. The symbols will work for you no matter what you do or don't do with your palms!

Why the symbols are there

At Second Degree, the prime focus of Reiki is still your self-healing, and the first two symbols are there to help you get to grips with two important energies that will further or deepen your self-healing. Putting the 'distant healing' symbol to one side, the other two symbols represent the energies of earth ki and heavenly ki, and we need to fully assimilate these two energies to enhance our self-healing and self-development. If we are going to use these energies when we treat other people, it makes sense to be thoroughly familiar with these energies, to have spent time 'becoming' these energies. We can do this by carrying out regular symbol meditations.

Making 'distant' connections

The third Reiki symbol that you are introduced to on a Second Degree course is commonly called the 'distant healing symbol'. We should remember that distant healing is perfectly possible at First Degree level and that we do not need to use a symbol in order to send Reiki to another person: intent is enough. But using this symbol can help us to learn to better 'click' into a nice strong merged state.

There is no set form of ritual that 'has' to be used in distant healing, there is not set form of words that has to be recited, no established sequence which needs to be reproduced in order for distant healing to be effective, so we can find our own comfortable approach, different from other people's but equally valid. The details of the ritual that we use are not important. All we need to do is to focus our attention on the recipient and maybe use the symbol in some way, merge with the energy, merge with the recipient, and allow the energy to flow.

Intuitive working

Ideally, Second Degree should be the stage where you start to leave the basic 'rulebook' behind and go 'freestyle', gearing your treatment towards the recipient's individual energy needs, so that each treatment will be different, as the recipient's energy needs change from one treatment session to another. Some students will already be modifying the basic treatment routine by the time that they arrive on their Second Degree course.

Set hand positions and a prescribed scheme to follow are useful things to have at First Degree, and allow the student to feel confident in treating others, but sequences of hand positions can be left behind when we open to intuition. Intuitive treatments seem to do something special for the recipient: when you direct the energy into just the right combination of positions for that person on that occasion you allow the energy to penetrate deeply and this seems to lead to a more profound experience for the recipient. Treatments using intuitively guided hand positions may involve much fewer hand positions being held, and each combination being held for much longer, than in a 'standard' treatment.

We recommend that the Japanese "Reiji ho" approach is used to help Second Degree students to open to their intuitive side, since the approach is so simple and seems to work for most people even within a few minutes of practice. The resulting strong belief that the student is "intuitive" is a hugely empowering state and opens many doors.

Finally

Reiki has the potential to make an amazing, positive difference to you and the people around you. Remember that Reiki is simplicity itself, and by taking some steps to work on yourself regularly, and share Reiki with the people close to you, you are embarking on a very special journey. How far you travel on that journey is governed by how many steps you take. Carry on with your Hatsurei and self-treatments, get to grips with the energies of CKR and SHK through regular meditation, find your own comfortable approach to carrying out distant healing, and open yourself to intuitive working. And have fun!

Notes

Notes

The Breath of Earth and Heaven

November 2003

In this article I would like to talk about the energy that we work with when we practise Reiki: when we work on ourselves and when we share Reiki with others. The energy that we channel is described in various ways: we are said to be working with universal energy, we are passing on unconditional love, or chi, or prana. But there are aspects of the energy that are not being explained through this use of words, and in this article I want to talk about the essence of Reiki energy. In doing this we will touch on Taoism, QiGong, Shintoism, meditation, breathing, chanting and the use of the Reiki symbols.

Now many people reading this article will be practising something called "Joshin Kokkyu Ho", an energy breathing method taught in the Usui Reiki Ryoho Gakkai, the Usui Memorial Society in Japan – part of a longer sequence of exercises referred to as "Hatsurei ho". It was also used in Mikao Usui's original system, according to a group of Usui Sensei's surviving students who are in contact with one or two people in the West. Joshin Kokkyu Ho translates as something like 'technique for purification of the spirit' or 'soul cleansing breathing method', and on its own 'Kokkyu Ho' means 'the way of breathing'. When we use this method we are moving energy in time with our breath, into and out of our Tanden (Dantien in Chinese), it is a way of achieving balance, but there is more significance to this technique than simply moving energy through our bodies.

With each in-breath we are filling the body with ki. This ki is yin in nature, it is the breath of earth, of physicality and the power of separation. By contrast the out-breath distributes ki throughout our bodies. This is yang in nature, it is the breath of heaven, of spirituality and the power of unification. So from the moment that we practise Joshin Kokkyu Ho we are experiencing earth ki and heavenly ki.

In fact, earth ki and heavenly ki are what we are: we are physical reality and we are spiritual essence. In Taoist philosophy, Earth and Heaven – along with Humanity – are known as the "Three Powers". Humanity is in a pivotal position between the cosmic powers of heaven and the natural forces of earth, covered by heaven above and supported by earth below. Qi Gong, the energy cultivation technique which is practised in Japan as 'kiko', allows us to work with these two energies and bring them into balance. Shinto practices also refer to these two basic energies, these two essential aspects of what we really are.

It is not surprising, then, that these two energies are the basis of Usui Sensei's spiritual system, and latterly his healing system. When we practise Reiki we are working with earth ki and heavenly ki, in a conscious or unconscious fashion; when we channel Reiki, we are channelling either the ki of earth or heaven, because that is what we are.

But Usui Sensei's system goes further than just acknowledging our true nature, our physical and spiritual nature, because Reiki allows us to fully experience our physical reality, and fully experience our spiritual essence. This is a powerful method for achieving balance. We can return to that state of perfection we enjoyed at birth, before life corrupted us; we can be reborn. How this was achieved is as follows: At second degree in the original system the student would be shown how to experience earth ki and heavenly ki, they would learn to 'become' the energies of earth and heaven. How this was achieved very much depended on the student's background, since Usui Sensei varied his teachings and methods according to the needs of his students. If the student had a Buddhist background then they would have used meditations, and if they had a Shinto background then they would have chanted sacred sounds called 'kotodama'. Later on in Usui's system, symbols were introduced for the Imperial Officers, but all these approaches had the same end in mind: to fully assimilate, to fully experience or become the energies of earth and heaven, the essence of what we are. The meditations, the kotodama, and the symbols are all tools used to trigger, to invoke within us, to allow us to experience an energy or a state. Second degree is all about getting to grips with earth ki and heavenly ki, to fully assimilate those energies, to reconnect to what is within and realise our true nature.

CKR and SHK represent earth ki and heavenly ki respectively, but they do not represent something new: these two energies are already within us. They do not represent something additional that we are connected to: they emphasise or flag up something that is already there.

Now, Usui Sensei's students worked long and hard to assimilate or integrate these energies. The might have spent 6-9 months just meditating on one energy, before moving on, so there were no short-cuts and it was a long process. They started with the energy of earth and moved on to work with the energy of heaven. We can echo that original practice by working with the energies of CKR and SHK. It is not enough to be 'attuned' to a symbol – whatever that means – and it is not enough to use a symbol in practice when treating someone. To fully get to grips with an energy we need to meditate on the symbol, using its energy individually, not combined with others, and we need to commit ourselves to doing this regularly if we are going to fully experience the benefits that are available through Usui Sensei's simple spiritual system.

Notes

Working with Intuition

August 2001

When I first started practising Reiki, I didn't believe that I was intuitive. In fact, I thought that I might only be able to become intuitive after years of dedicated practice, if then. I thought that maybe intuition was only for the gifted few, or if it did arrive for me then it would flash into my head, gone in an instant, and I would not know how to get it back again.

I now realise that intuition is available for everyone, right from the word go, and that by doing just a few simple things we can all amaze ourselves with what we can become aware of. Partly I have come to this conclusion through trial and error, and partly through practising an intuitive technique called 'Reiji ho' that is used in Japanese-style Reiki, a technique that allows your hands to be moved 'by invisible magnets' to the right places to treat. I have a long way to go with intuition: it is a lifelong journey, but I thought some people might find my experiences and experimentation interesting to read about...

For a while I used to use a pendulum when I treated people. I had agreed with the pendulum what it would do if a chakra was closed, spinning too fast, or 'normal', and I would dangle the pendulum over each chakra in turn and ask 'show me the state of the crown chakra', and so on along the length of the body. Some people ask if each chakra in turn is balanced, others dangle the pendulum and watch its direction of rotation and size of circle traced out, showing how the chakra spins and how open it is. I found after a while that I did not need to hold the pendulum over the chakra; I could just hold the pendulum at my side and ask it as the client lay in front of me. Then I discovered that I did not need to have the client in front of me either, and that I could balance their chakras before they arrived for a treatment! I was starting to realise that there were not too many limits to this technique.

On occasion I forgot to bring my pendulum with me, and I could not find anything to use as a substitute, so I started using an 'imaginary pendulum' which I 'held'. My arm made the same muscle movements as before, without the need to suspend a crystal from a thread. Some people use a pendulum that swings 'in their imagination'. They watch to see how its spin changes in response to their questions. I don't get on very well with that: I never seem to be able to look at the pendulum from the right angle to tell exactly what it is doing!

I tried to move on from this to see if I could dispense with a pendulum altogether, whether real or imaginary. I started 'looking' at someone's chakras by imagining a series of seven circles one above another, and looking at each circle in turn to see whether it was small and closed, or open and large. I did not trust this to begin with, of course, because I thought 'this is just my imagination... I am making this up', so I went back to my trusted imaginary pendulum, and was amazed to find that the pendulum agreed with my 'imagination'.

On an update day for my Reiki Masters we practised visualising each other's chakras, and there was a whole variety of presentations. One person saw traffic lights with lights at different intensities. One saw a string of seven beads. Another could not see anything until she 'peered' over the edge of the chakra, to look down on a lotus flower; some of the flowers had petals that were folded in, others had their petals fully open.

Eventually I moved on from the pendulum, and the imaginary pendulum, and used an imaginary 'mixing desk', rather like you might see in a recording studio: a series of seven vertical 'sliders' with a central point that represents 'balance'. I looked at each chakra slider in turn and if it slid downwards then the chakra was closed or spinning sluggishly, and if it moved upwards then the chakra was spinning too fast.

Now I realise that I do not need to perceive someone's chakras, except out of interest, and certainly I do not need to do anything by way of using Reiki to ‘balance’ the chakras: Reiki works on the recipient’s energy system to achieve more of a state of balance, on all levels, so Reiki works on people’s chakras without my having to do anything specific to help, other than by standing by and being a clear channel.

But my experimentation showed me that I was intuitive, that I could trust my intuition, and that I did not need to use ‘props’: the intuition was there, the intuitive message was there, and the pendulum (or the imaginary pendulum) was just a tool to use to access what was already there within me.

The Japanese connection to all this comes in the form of an intuitive 'technique' called "Reiji Ho" which means something like 'indication of the spirit technique'. Details of this method have come to us through Frank Arjava Petter and Hiroshi Doi, and information from Usui's surviving students suggests that this method was probably taught to the Imperial Officers by Usui Sensei. This method involves allowing the energy to guide your hands to the right places to treat, so rather than following the Western system of 'standard hand positions' you allow Reiki to put your hands in the right place for each person you treat. You are then gearing your treatment to the individual's energy needs, rather than applying a 'rubber stamp' treatment to everyone. People who I have treated using both approaches have found that intuitive treatments seem to penetrate more deeply, seem more relevant to them and more profound. Once this technique is mastered then every treatment is different: the hand positions change from one person to another and from one treatment to another with the same client, based on their individual needs. Intuitive treatments are liberating; you just merge with the energy and let it happen!

This was the basis for Usui's original method: letting the energy guide you.

I have described Reiji Ho as a technique, yet in fact there is no method. The 'technique' involves not doing, not thinking, not trying; in fact it works best if you can simply get your mind out of the way completely. You feel your connection with the energy, feel the energy flowing through you, and as you do so imagine yourself joining with the energy, merging with the energy, becoming one with the energy... and you simply allow the energy to guide your hands.

What is so exciting for me is that this technique works for almost everyone within a few minutes, so of the 260+ people who have been taught this technique on my 'Original Usui Reiki' update course, more than 95% have found that it works for them almost immediately. I teach this technique routinely on my Reiki 2 courses and it works incredibly well. The Japanese 'Reiju' empowerments seem to have the effect of giving people greater intuitive potential, so the combination of Reiju and Reiji ho, as well as the energy exercises called Hatsu Rei Ho, work very well together, fitting like the pieces of a simple and elegant jigsaw. What is also exciting is that if you make it a basic part of your Reiki practice to open yourself to intuition, then you will develop additional intuitive abilities, so moving your hands is only the starting point!

It is liberating and exciting to realise that intuition is there from the start, and that all you have to do to access that inner knowledge is to suspend your disbelief, trust that it will work for you, and have a go. Don't try hard, don't force it, and don't think about it... just merge with the energy, empty your head, and let it happen!

Notes

Notes

The Importance of Intent

May 2002

A wise friend of mine once said to me that "where thought goes, energy flows" and I think that this principle applies very well to Reiki. Some of us have been taught in quite a rigid way, learning that we must always follow a particular prescription to achieve a desired effect, whether this be a set form of words, a collection of symbols, or a complicated ritual. That's fine: we can choose to do that if we like, but I believe that underlying our form of words, our rituals and our symbols is an important and powerful driving force: our intention. I believe that we can move beyond the details, the constructed systems, to access that simple, profound and powerful controlling force. Whatever we do, when we do Reiki, we control the energy using our intention.

Many people are now experimenting with sending Reiki using their eyes and their breath, based on the two Japanese techniques 'Gyoshi Ho' and 'Koki Ho'. Now I do not believe that Reiki necessarily comes out of your eyeballs when you use the 'eye' technique, like Clark Kent raising his glasses to send laser beams out of his eyes. But I do think that you have created a little visualisation that sends the energy in a particular way. When you imagine that Reiki passes from your eyes, the energy is focused in a way that picks up on some of the connotations of staring: the energy is received in a piercing, localised, penetrating, or 'focused' way. Send using your breath and the energy is sent in more of a superficial 'billowing' form.

You have made the energy go to the other person's body. You have intended that, and it has happened. You visualised to achieve this, but that is just a convenient way of focusing your intent, and it is your intent that is the important thing here, not the details of the ritual that you use to control the energy.

You may choose to carry out a detailed ritual in order to perform distant healing, you may use a set form of words, a symbol, more symbols, you may make a detailed visualisation, but you are still focusing your intent and the details of the ritual don't matter. If you feel comfortable with detailed ritual - 'High Church' - then fine, that works for you; stick with that. But I think we need to realise that we can remove the strait jacket, we can let the ritual go if we want to and still achieve the desired effect, and that is still Reiki.

We can experiment: sit a Reiki friend the other side of the room and send Reiki to their forehead, or their shoulder. Don't beam it, don't do distant healing, don't use your eyes or your hands: sit on your hands, close your eyes and just *make* the energy go where you want. It will follow your thoughts. When you are thinking nice warm thoughts about another person then dzzzzt, the energy has followed your thoughts, your focus, and you have just sent distant healing to them.

When we self-treat we can move the energy through our bodies using our mind, using our intention. If you can't contort yourself and get your hands to rest on the part that you want to treat, just imagine that your hands are resting on the area that you want to treat, and the energy will be there. If you have backache, and you were lying on your bed with your hands resting on your abdomen, you could imagine - visualise - that the energy was flowing from your hands to your back, and the energy would go there. You can even 'cut out the middle man': draw down the energy through your crown and imagine it passing through your body to the affected area. The energy will go there.

The symbols, too, are a visual focus that connects us to a particular aspect of the energy that is already within us. Usui introduced symbols late on in Reiki's history for the benefit of the Imperial Officers who trained with him. They are the foundation of Western Reiki, though not of the 'original' form of Reiki that Usui Sensei taught to most of his students. We can go beyond the symbols too if we feel that we want to, once we have experienced the distinctive flavours, the distinctive energies, of the Reiki symbols. Unfortunately the Western way does not tend to give us this opportunity, but the potential is there. What lies behind each symbol is a distinctive, characteristic energy, and with practice we can move the symbol to one side and access the energies direct if we choose, and that is still Reiki.

We can limit our practice of Reiki with our belief. If we believe that something is not possible, or not 'correct', then we are shooting ourselves in the foot before we even begin. If we believe that something is not possible then we will not try, we will not maximise our potential, and our Reiki is diminished as a result. If we can raise our horizons, suspend our disbelief, and simply try things, then we will be amazed by what is possible, and how simple things can be.

"Where thought goes, energy flows."

Notes

Remote Treatments

February 2003

When is a distant healing session not a distant healing session? ... When it is a remote treatment! What is a remote treatment? Well that is what I hope to describe in this article, and I also want to talk a little bit about 'removing the barriers' when you treat someone, going freestyle; I will outline some of the things that are possible when you simply suspend your disbelief, and try things out to see what's possible.

Now distant healing is based on the idea of making a long-distance 'connection' with the recipient, maybe by using a symbol, maybe by using a sacred sound, or maybe simply when you still your mind and you find that space where you are 'at one', merging with the other person. Your 'connection' to the recipient is a state of mind, a matter of your intention, and the details of the ritual that you use are not important.

Some Reiki people are taught that they need to keep at least one hand on the recipient at all times when they carry out hands-on treatments - otherwise they'll 'lose the connection' - but of course you are 'connected' to the recipient just as much when your hands are hovering away from the body. Your 'connection' does not depend on the physical proximity of your hands to someone's body. You are connected with your intention, when you are still and focused, you are connected as soon as you direct your attention towards the recipient.

But let's get back to distant healing. In practice this tends to be carried out for 10-15 minutes at a time over a number of consecutive days, and we send the energy to the person for their highest good, in a 'general' way, not directing the energy to a particular area.

But since our 'connection' to the person is a state of mind, we could maintain that 'distant' connection for a prolonged period if we wanted, and we could direct the energy with our intention to different specific parts of the recipient's body, in the same way that when we treat someone we direct the energy with our hands to specific areas of the body. And since with Reiki the energy follows our thoughts, it follows our focus; we can direct the energy using visualisation, which is a convenient shortcut to focus our intent.

So we can if we like carry out a ''remote treatment', where we maintain our connection to the recipient for maybe 30-40 minutes and direct the energy into the recipient's body by using imaginary hand positions. The energy will enter the recipient's body in the areas we imagine/intend. What hand positions should we use? Well we could go through a set of 'standard' hand positions, but we should learn to move beyond that as soon as we can. Far better to use our intuition, and a good way of working out where our hands should go is to use the Japanese intuitive 'technique' called "Reiji Ho".

"Reiji ho" is basically a way of getting your head out of the way, merging with the energy and allowing your hands to move, rather like having your hands moved by invisible magnets. Just like dowsing or automatic writing, Reiji Ho allows us to tap in to subconscious knowledge, and that knowledge is expressed through muscle movements. We already know the best places to put our hands, but quite often our mind gets in the way and stops us from getting to that deep knowing. Reiji helps to get our head out of the way for us.

So once you are connected to the other person in your mind, you can imagine them lying down on a treatment couch and visualise imaginary hands resting on or hovering over them. In your mind's eye, 'look' at your hands and see where they want to drift. They will drift in your mind's eye; be neutral, simply interested to see where they come to rest. When they come to rest, direct Reiki into your subject in those areas using intent; imagine energy flooding through those imaginary hands into the recipient's body. The energy will enter the recipient's body in the places that you imagine.

How long should you keep your hands in a particular position? Maybe you have a feeling that you ought to move on to a different position, but you're not sure whether you should yet. Here's a way to see if you should move on: in your mind's eye, pull one of your imaginary hands away from the place where it was resting; if it wants to slip back to that place again, rather like it was attached by an elastic band, then you can stay there for longer, directing the energy into the body in that position until you feel that the imaginary hand will drift away easily. This visualisation can be used when you are doing hands-on treatments too, to let you know whether it's ok to move on to the next hand position.

Then 'see' where your imaginary hands want to drift next, and direct energy into your 'remote treatment' recipient using your visualisation or intent. This is a lovely way to work, because you have to really merge with the energy, to become one with the energy, to do this.

In fact you can even 'scan' the recipient at a distance if you want. Hover one hand in mid-air, palm down, and in your mind's eye imagine your hand drift over the recipient's body. Notice the areas where there seems to be a lot of energy flowing in your hand. Try it. It works!

So why don't you try an experiment: get a willing victim to lie down at a prearranged time for, say, 45 minutes. Connect to them in your head, using your intent, let the energy guide your imaginary hands, direct the energy using visualisation (using intent) and see what you perceive. Go with the flow. See what they notice. Suspend your disbelief and see what happens!

Notes

Symbols, Attunements and Beyond

August 2000

In the Western style of Reiki, the Reiki symbols are seen to be very important. They are seen as an integral part of the system; indeed for many people the symbols **are** Reiki, the symbols **are** the energy. It has been a basic tenet of Western Reiki that you have to be 'attuned' to the symbols for them to work for you and that you are connected to Reiki only when you have been 'attuned' to the symbols. All Western style attunement systems – as far as I can see – involve being attuned to symbols at First Degree, Second Degree and Master levels. However, no one really knew if you needed to be attuned to the symbols for them to work for you, and no one really knew whether symbols needed to enter into the connection ritual used, because no one knew of a way to attune people without using symbols! The only connection rituals that we had were attunements, and all attunements used symbols!

But new information coming from Japan, and the experiences of some Reiki people experimenting in the West, suggest that the Reiki symbols might not be such a necessary part of 'attuning' people as was once thought, and suggest that there is no need for a person to be 'attuned' to a symbol for it to work for them, so long as they are already connected to Reiki.

Now, we now know that Mikao Usui did not teach symbols to the vast majority of his students, and those few students who were taught symbols (the Imperial Officers) were not 'attuned' to these symbols by Usui Sensei. In fact, Mikao Usui did not attune anybody to anything: he used to 'empower' his students, and the empowerments that he bestowed on his students, at all levels, did not utilise the Reiki symbols.

So where did attunements come from, and where did the idea of 'attuning' someone to symbols in order for the student to be 'connected' to Reiki, and to be able to use those symbols, come from? Well it seems certain that the Imperial Officers had not trained with Usui Sensei for long enough before he died for them to have been taught by him how to empower students (Usui taught this quite far along on the Master student's journey). Usui did not attune people and he did not teach attunements. So it seems that the Imperial Officers developed for themselves a ritual – an 'attunement' - by way of trying to replicate the experiences that they had had when being empowered by Usui Sensei, and because they had been taught symbols, these symbols entered into the ritual that they developed.

A version of this ritual was passed from Dr Hayashi (one of the Imperial Officers) to Mrs Takata, who passed on a ritual to her Master students, and the ritual has now been endlessly distorted and embellished as it has been passed from teacher to teacher in the West.

Interestingly, Hiroshi Doi – a member of the Usui Reiki Ryoho Gakkai (Usui Memorial Society, set up after his death by some of the Imperial Officers) – has said that the 'attunement' methods used in the 'Gakkai do not involve the use of symbols: the 'Gakkai's students are connected to Reiki, but the Reiki symbols are not used in this process. Mr Doi also said that Mikao Usui introduced the symbols for the benefit of students who could just not accept that they could 'do this thing', and by giving them something concrete to use, they learned to focus and control the energy more easily.

Hiroshi Doi also says that the current 'Gakkai students do not use the Reiki symbols, though they are shown them out of historical interest. Mikao Usui no doubt chose the symbols very carefully, to represent different aspects of the energy, but the energy and the connection to the energy came first.

But let's go back to the empowerments that Usui was using: the empowerments bestowed by Usui Sensei could be referred to as "Reiju", a Tendai Buddhist blessing made with the intention that the student should 'receive what they need', and a form of Reiju has been passed to us via Mikao Usui's surviving students. Reiju is a way of 'connecting' you to Reiki, though all such rituals really do (whether attunements of empowerments) is to help you recognise something that is already there: they do not connect you to something external to you that you were not connected to before. Reiju – at all levels – does not involve using symbols, at all. So Reiju is a way of 'connecting' someone to Reiki but without any symbols entering into the process. And thus we have a way of demonstrating, for the first time, that 'attuning' someone to a symbol is not a necessary step in 'connecting' them to Reiki.

This is quite a revelation for the world of Western-style Reiki.

Not only that, but now that we know how to connect people to Reiki without using symbols, and without 'attuning' people to symbols, we can at last find out whether one needs to be attuned to a symbol for it to work for us.

Several years ago I experimented...

I found, for example, that students attuned at First Degree level, using Western-style attunements, can produce noticeable effects in their hands when using the Reiki symbols; they can use the symbols, experience their energies and channel the energies that the symbols represent. Western-style Reiki First Degree attunements use the Reiki symbols, of course, but you are not usually 'attuned' to them in the way that you are at Second Degree level, and First Degree students are not 'supposed' to be able to use the Reiki symbols, or carry out things like distant healing (though, of course, this is nonsense).

I also found that the symbols work just as well for First Degree students who are connected to Reiki using Reiju empowerments, (the symbol-free connection ritual). In fact, I have noticed that students attuned using Reiju seem to be more sensitive to the flow of Reiki than students attuned in the Western style.

Taking this one stage further, I have been using Reiju empowerments with students at Second Degree level, students who were 'connected' using Reiju at First Degree too, and found that students attuned in this way can use the Reiki symbols in just the same way, and just as effectively, as students attuned using the Western system... although these students have not been 'attuned' to the symbols.

So all this leads me to believe that once you have been connected to Reiki – and we now know that symbols do not need to enter into this process – then the Reiki symbols will work for you, and you do not need to be 'attuned' to them specifically (whatever that means). Not only that, but I believe that **any** symbol will direct the energy in a particular way once you have been attuned to Reiki: Usui's chosen symbols which come from Shintoism and Tendai Buddhism, but also symbols from other cultures and traditions, and channelled symbols too.

I have personal experience of this, and so do my students. Channelled symbols, for example, can be used effectively by people who have not been 'attuned' to them; they can be shown them, meditate on them and experience their characteristic energies. I have been in contact with a Moldovan Doctor (and Reiki Master) whose Reiki friends use Christian symbols to control and focus the Reiki energy. I also know a Moslem Reiki Master who uses Moslem prayers to frame the energy in a particular way, and he can feel the energy altering its nature as the prayer is recited.

In Usui Sensei's original system, sacred sounds called 'kotodama' were taught as a way of experiencing, and directing, the energy. Students were not 'attuned' to a kotodama (however that might have been achieved): they simply used the sound and the sound moulded the energy.

The Reiki symbols are simply graphical representations of different aspects of the energy. You can simply look at them, remember them and use them and they will work for you, whether or not you have been through some sort of ritual that involved the teacher visualising them as they 'connected' you.

From personal experience, and the experience of many Reiki people, I can say that it is possible to produce the desired effect with the energy through intent only, whether that be distant healing or gearing the energy in the direction of mental/emotional balancing or physical healing.

So for me there is a distinction to be made between the energy of Reiki and any graphics (symbols) that might be used to control and focus the energy in a particular way. Reiki is the energy, you are 'connected' to the energy, but symbols do not need to enter into the connection process for it to work, nor do you need to have been 'attuned' to a symbol before it will work for you. There are many ways of directing the energy: by using symbols from Japan or from other cultures or sources, by using sound, and through simple intent.

Notes

Simplicity and Sandwiches

February 2002

In the West, there seems to be this insidious tendency to make things unnecessarily complicated, almost on the basis that if it's more complicated, it is better. We have to take things and make them bigger and better; we have to add stuff. In Japan, of course, they seem to go in the opposite direction, paring things down to the bone, getting rid of any unnecessary frills and flounces, leaving us with the pure essence of a thing, simple and elegant. Think of Japanese garden design, flower arranging, the tea ceremony, and you will see what I mean.

This contrast can be seen in the practices of Western Reiki and original Japanese Reiki.

Western attunements, for example, tend to be quite complicated affairs. There are lots of different Western ways of connecting you to Reiki, some of them quite contradictory in terms of the way that they are supposed to work, but they do all work. Some have lots of puffing and blowing; some are more restrained. Some have lots of tapping and patting, others don't, some attune your hands, and some attune your fingertips. Some have different rituals at Reiki1, Reiki2 and Master levels, while others have exactly the same rituals but you repeat the process a different number of times at the different levels. They all involve your head: they are busy, you are drawing symbols, saying names, putting things in different places, saying various affirmations in your head and imagining things.

The Japanese approach is rather different. The way that Mikao Usui empowered people was simplicity itself, and his surviving students are passing on a simple, elegant connection ritual called 'Reiju", which is a way of conveying what Usui Sensei bestowed on his students. Reiju is the same in its form at all levels and is a lovely energy dance, rather like following the flowing form of Tai Chi or Qigong. Reiju is not a 'head' activity, because you simply merge yourself with the energy and follow the form. It is a real pleasure to carry out, as anyone who has learned it will attest. Reiju is pure simplicity.

In some Western lineages there are rigid sets of hand positions that you have to follow, in all treatments. Some people are taught that not only must they always use these 'correct' hand positions, but they must also spend a set amount of time in each hand position. They move their hands like robots from one position to another on hearing a 'bell' on one of a number of special CDs used as a guide. Yet Usui's method took a simpler approach: rather than following a standard set of hand positions, you were expected to work at developing your intuition so that your hands were moved by the energy to the right places to treat. The hand positions you used would change from one person to another, and from one treatment to another within the same person, based on their individual energy needs; a simple and elegant approach, free from dogma and rigidity.

But it is in the use of the Reiki symbols, the Reiki energies, where there is perhaps the greatest gulf between Usui's original method and the techniques used in the West. In the West, Second Degree Reiki involves being 'attuned' to three symbols, two that can be used when giving treatments and a third used in the 'sending' of Reiki long-distance. These were not 'new' symbols that were introduced to the world by Usui after a moment of enlightenment, as the Mrs Takata-inspired history of Reiki tells us, but existing symbols that he appropriated into his system quite late in Reiki's history.

Depending on what lineage we have, we are taught different ways of using these symbols. In one lineage you may be taught to use all three symbols in each and every hand position when you are treating someone. Another lineage will tell you that the second symbol is hardly ever to be used, or is only to be used in a narrow and predefined set of circumstances. In most lineages the first symbol is seen as some sort of 'power' symbol that doesn't seem to do much on its own but makes other symbols stronger, and you are taught to put the symbols on top of each other, or mix them together. Some people have developed quite complicated arrangements where you use one symbol, and then put another on top, and then another one, and then another one, and so on. This technique has been called the 'Reiki sandwich'. But are these approaches an unnecessary complication, and could there be a simpler approach that might be more effective in practice?

We Westerners seem to focus more on the Reiki symbols than in Japan. For example, according to Hiroshi Doi, the Usui Reiki Ryoho Gakkai ('Usui's Reiki Healing Association') does not use the Reiki symbols. Students are shown the symbols out of historical interest, but they are expected to work directly with the energies that the symbols represent. We also know that most of the people that Mikao Usui taught were not given symbols, but used other approaches to connect to the energies that in the West we use the symbols to represent.

What is interesting too is the way that Usui had his students use these energies, because it challenges the Western way of using symbols. Rather than being some sort of 'power symbol', the first energy was seen as focusing on the physical body, it was seen as a physical healing energy. This was the solid energy of earth. The second energy was seen as producing harmony, it was celestial energy, working on the thoughts and emotions, the energy of our spiritual essence, a bit like the second symbol/energy is seen in the West. So now we have energies that will deal with healing the body, and the mind / emotions / spirit, the whole spectrum.

Not only that, but these energies were used individually, on their own, not mixed endlessly with other energies and symbols in complicated arrangements and sequences. You chose an energy using your intuition, and you focused on it. By focusing on one thing, rather than trying to do lots of things at the same time, you intensify the effect. Isn't that simple?

Notes

A Simple Way with Symbols

August 2002

In the West we like to make things complicated, and the way that most of us now use symbols is a world away from the simple approach that Usui used. So how can we work with symbols in a way that echoes more the way that Usui taught his students?

Well firstly, Usui taught symbols to a very small number of people, just in the last few years of his life. The vast majority of his students were taught in a very different way. Most of his students were given meditations to use so that they could, over a long period of time, become more and more familiar with the three energies taught at second-degree level, for example. Once they were thoroughly familiar with the energies, once they had *become* the energies again and again, then they were given a shortcut – a trigger – to connect them to those energies. The triggers that they used were ancient Shinto mantras called kotodama or jumon, not symbols.

In the West we do it backwards by comparison: we are given a trigger (a symbol) to connect us to an energy that we are not familiar with, and with which we may never become familiar, depending on how we have been taught to use the symbols. Usui had his students become the three energies again and again and again, and when they were ingrained, when they were innate, only then would you be given a way of connecting to the energies that were already within you and thoroughly familiar to you.

The energies were also viewed somewhat differently. The first energy was not seen as some sort of 'Power' energy, in the way that the first symbol is seen as the 'Power' symbol in the West. The first energy was simply earth energy, energy of the physical body, a physical healing energy. The second energy was seen as heavenly energy and the third energy was said to produce 'oneness'. Usui's students learned to get to grips with these energies through meditation, so how can we learn to experience earth energy and celestial energy? Well we can do this by using the symbols...

Try this solitary exercise: sit comfortably in a chair with your eyes closed and your hands resting in your lap palms uppermost. In your mind's eye, visualise the first symbol up in the air above you, and say its name silently to yourself three times. Now imagine that cascades of energy are flooding down onto you from that symbol, cascading into your head, your torso, your hands; endless cascades of energy or light keep on flooding into your body, flowing over you and flooding through you. Do this for several minutes. How does that feel? What impressions do you get of the energy? Where was your attention focused? What were your thoughts?

Now repeat this exercise using the second symbol, again visualising it up in the air above you, saying its name three times, and drawing down endless cascades of energy into your body. How does this feel by comparison? What impressions do you get of the second energy? Where is your attention focused? What is going on in your head?

If you have a Reiki friend to hand, you can do this exercise together: one person sits comfortably in a chair and the other stands behind. The person standing up is going to send energy from the first or second symbol in quite an intense way. What they do is this: 'charge' your hands with the energy of the first symbol, say, by drawing the symbol over your palm, saying the name three times, and press your hands together to 'transfer the effect across' to he other hand. Now in your mind's eye draw out the first symbol up in the air above you and say the name three times. Move your hands so that they are hovering alongside the recipient's temples, and imagine that you are drawing down cascades of energy from the symbol above you, which flood into your crown, through your arms and out of your hands into the recipient. Keep on visualising. How does the energy feel as it comes through your hands? What impressions do you get in your body? How does it feel for the recipient? What adjectives can they use to describe the essence of the energy that they have received?

Now repeat this exercise using the second symbol. How does this differ from the first energy?

Having carried out this exercise countless times and with many, many students, I can generalise about the sort of impression that most people tend to get from the two symbols, the two energies. Maybe you will notice some, though not all, of these experiences.

The first energy seems thick, dark, heavy, dense, solid, maybe oppressive or claustrophobic sometimes, hot, fierce, coarse, penetrating, with pressure and slow pulsation, your focus is on your physical body. The second energy seems soft, light, gentle, ethereal, like soft fluffy clouds or marshmallows, cool, blue, expansive, exhilarating, and uplifting.

What you have experienced is the essence of earth energy and the essence of heavenly energy, and these are two energies that you have available to you when treating others. These energies are the essence of Usui's system at second-degree level. The first energy focuses on the physical body, and the second focuses on thoughts and emotions and our spiritual nature. They are so different, so distinctive. Try using them on their own, just one energy, just one focus, without mixing symbols together. Keep things simple and uncluttered by focusing like a laser beam on one thing at a time, and see what happens. And with time, and with familiarity with the two energies, try producing those energies directly, using intent, and see what happens.

Notes

Feng Shui your Reiki

May 2003

Many of you will be familiar with Feng Shui, the Oriental art of placement, where you arrange your living environment to allow smooth flow of chi through your home, eliminating areas where chi will stagnate, and slowing down the speed of fast-rushing chi. So what has that to do with Reiki? Well they both deal with chi, but what I am really thinking of is applying the basic principles of Feng Shui to our practice of Reiki. This may seem a little strange, but please bear with me...

The basic principle of Feng Shui, the first thing you have to do before you do anything else, is to get rid of your clutter, because a cluttered environment leads to a cluttered life. Only once you have rid yourself of your unnecessary bits and pieces should you move in to apply the other more specific principles of placement. So could we de-clutter our practice of Reiki, what would that be like, and how could we achieve that? Is our Reiki cluttered now? How could we pare it down to the essentials and leave the unnecessary stuff behind?

We do seem to have a tendency in the West to make things endlessly complicated, almost on the basis that if it's more complicated then it's better. We like to introduce rules and regulations and restrictions and dogma, maybe because rules make us feel supported and safe, or maybe because we just can't leave a simple thing alone! Yet the system that Usui Sensei taught to his surviving students wasn't complicated. It wasn't cluttered. It was simple and elegant and profound, and I think that we've drifted away from that in many ways. We've introduced rules and restrictions and dogma into many aspects of Reiki practice: connecting to the energy, treating someone, hand positions, distant healing methods, situations where you 'should not treat'. This is all clutter and we can do without it. Freeing ourselves from this burden of technique and method and limitation would be a great and beneficial clear-out. We don't need it. It holds us back. Let's look at a few examples of unnecessary clutter…

A while ago I was contacted by a poor girl who had been taught that she needed to go through a fifteen-stage ritual in order to 'connect' to Reiki. She and the other students on the course were quite worried, obviously concerned that if they didn't get all the stages right then the energy wouldn't come through properly and their treatments would be ineffective. Naturally they wanted to do the very best they could for the people they were working on, and they were focusing hard on getting all the necessary stages right.

Yet 'connection' with Reiki is simply a state of mind; you connect when you intend to connect. Some people will hold their hands in a particular position (hands above them with palms uppermost to the sky, hands to the sides with palms face up, hands in the prayer position, hands in their lap with palms up, hands folded over the Dantien). Maybe they will say a set form of words, but all these are optional. Bring the energy through your crown to your Dantien and bathe in the light, flood the energy through your body, be still; you are connected when you intend to be. It is a matter of focus, a matter of where your attention lies.

Some people are taught that they must always keep one of their hands in contact with the recipient when they treat, based on the idea that if you take both hands off then you have lost your connection to the recipient and the energy will not flow properly. But your connection to the recipient is a state of mind too: you focus your attention on them, you merge with them and become one with them, and that is sufficient no matter what you are doing with your hands. In fact your treatment starts as soon as you are standing by the table with your attention directed towards the person. Your treatment has already started when you are scanning, or feeling the energy field. Reiki works just as well when you have your hands off the body, though Reiki is basically practised as a hands-on method.

Some Reiki people are taught rigid 'standard' hand positions that have to be used every time you treat, and there is the view that if you are not using 'the' hand positions then you haven't been taught properly. Some even have a rigid time limit that has to be followed, so you can only keep your hands in each position for so many minutes… you can buy Reiki CDs which make a little 'ping' sound every three minutes (or whatever), and everyone changes hand positions like a robot. Yet what if your hands are going like crazy, what if there energy needs to flood into a particular area for a long time and you need to keep your hands there for 5 minutes or 10 minutes or 15 minutes? The answer would seem to be that you follow the system rigidly and ignore your hands. How sad.

Now standard hand positions are useful when you first learn Reiki: it's reassuring to have some sort of system to follow. But we can move beyond those standard hand positions in a couple of ways. When we 'scan' the body we night discover areas that are drawing lots of Reiki, but they aren't covered by the 'standard' hand positions… we can alter our hand positions accordingly, or add extra positions, to make sure we're directing the energy into the areas that are drawing the most Reiki. We can use intuition, too, to control our hand positioning, and this has great benefits for the recipient because we are directing the energy into just the right combination of positions for each person we are working on. We might feel inexplicably 'drawn' to a particular area, we might just 'know' that we ought to be treating a particular area, or we might be practicing "Reiji Ho" from Japan, where our hands are drawn by 'invisible magnets' to the right areas to treat. Again we are leaving the rigid standard positions to one side and going with the flow. That was Usui's way: there were no real standard positions. You simply put your hands where they wanted to go.

Distant healing is another area where lots of rules and regulations have crept in over time. Some people are taught quite complicated rituals that they have to carry out when they perform distant healing, with a set form of words that 'have' to be used in a particular way, and with various required visualisations. Yet the bare bones of distant healing are to know where the energy is to go – to set a firm intent – to use the distant healing symbol maybe, and to merge with the recipient, allowing the energy to flow. Anything beyond that is optional. People have different styles: some like to actively visualise and develop a detailed ritual, and that's fine, but it's not actually necessary. Others like to keep it simple, and that works just as well. Even the use of the distant healing symbol is optional, though it does help us to focus on merging with the recipient, a way of experiencing 'oneness' with the person you're sending the energy to. Distant healing is perfectly possible at First Degree level, too: it's simple a matter of intent, of focusing your attention in a particular way. The energy follows your thoughts, it follows your focus.

The final area where we could give our Reiki a big 'clear out' is in the rules and restrictions that can control who we should and should not treat. Some people are given a long list of 'contraindications': situations where you should not give Reiki because it might be dangerous. Some contraindications that I have come across include: pregnant women, babies, people with pacemakers, diabetics*, people undergoing an anaesthetic, people wearing contact lenses, people with cancer, people suffering from stress, people with broken bones, people taking homoeopathic remedies, people undergoing chemotherapy, people with a torn muscle. There will be many more examples taught in different lineages. These restrictions are nonsense, they have no basis: there is no proper evidence – even anecdotes – to back up the restrictions that are taught in some lineages. Reiki is safe, the person's body draws it to the right areas to treat, and Reiki is seen as divinely inspired, intelligent, it is seen as pure unconditional love. That view hardly sits too well with the suggestion that you can hurt someone using Reiki. We think too much, we worry too much, and we create problems where there are none.

So a practice of Reiki that follows the first principle of Feng Shui will be a simple practice, free from rules, restrictions and self-imposed limitations. Feng Shui'd Reiki will be free from dogma, and free from rituals that you 'must' follow for Reiki to work effectively. It will be a practice that is based on simple intent and intuition, where you merge with the recipient, where you become one with them, and where you let the energy guide you. Let's get rid of all that clutter and free up our practice, and just let the energy flow.

*[* There is some anecdotal evidence that some diabetics may experience a short term alteration in blood sugar levels following a Reiki treatment. They should be made aware of this possibility and monitor their sugar levels accordingly. However, this does not mean that you should not treat diabetics using Reiki, as is suggested in some quarters. It just means that diabetics should keep an eye on their blood sugar levels following a Reiki treatment or a course of Reiki treatments. They should be checking their blood sugar levels routinely in any case.]*

Notes

Finally

The 10 Rules of Reiki

February 2007

In this article I thought I would set down ten things that you can do – ten principles to take account of – to benefit your practice of Reiki. This is not something that has come from Japan, or from early practitioners of Reiki: it is just something that I have put together myself. I hope that this article will be of interest to people at all Reiki levels.

(1) Reiki is all about you

Although Reiki is sometimes presented in the West as a sort of complementary therapy, a hands-on treatment technique, or a form of Japanese spiritual healing, that is not what Reiki is all about. If your practice of Reiki consists mainly of treating other people then you are missing the point because Reiki is all about you! Reiki is a personal practice for your self-healing and your spiritual and self-development. You are the priority here.

In Usui's time the treatment of others was not focused upon or emphasised, in fact treatments were a bit of a distraction from the main thrust of his teachings, which Usui Sensei referred to as a "system to achieve personal perfection". Right from the start, the system was about personal development, not working on others.

So to gain the greatest benefits for yourself through Reiki, you need to establish a decent routine of working on yourself in whatever way that you were taught. If you were taught

Western-style then do your hands-on self-treatment regularly, if you know about Japanese-style Reiki then practise your Hatsurei ho; if you know about Usui Sensei's original system then add his self-treatment meditation to your regular Hatsurei.

I know that some people seem to have the view that working on yourself is in some way 'selfish', but if you cannot look after yourself properly then how can you help other people? By working on yourself regularly you make yourself a better channel and more effective at what you do in terms of treatments, so there are plus points all round for those who make themselves their Reiki priority.

(2) Base your practice on the precepts

Usui Sensei established a simple spiritual system that was rooted in his precepts, his 'rules to live by'. Rather than being an interesting set of instructions to read on a course and put to one side, Usui's precepts are at the very heart of his system, and it was said that as much spiritual development could come through following the precepts as would come through doing any of the energy work. If we are consider ourselves as 'practising Reiki' then we will follow the precepts.

So we need to think deeply about the precepts and how they affect our lives. We need to consider each precept in turn and reflect on how that precept might impinge upon and guide our thoughts and behaviour and relationships and priorities. And we need to do this regularly, using the precepts as an ongoing source of guidance, the effects of which will make a real difference to us, and the people around us, over time.

The precepts are something that you we drip-feed into our lives, something that we refer to regularly and reflect on regularly, for our own benefit and for the benefit of the people with whom we come into contact.

(3) Practise mindfulness

Although not referred to on most Reiki courses, the practise of mindfulness was as important part of Usui Sensei's system as were the precepts, and in fact mindfulness is hidden in the precepts! Mindfulness is a form of meditation that one can perform at any time, when carrying out ordinary, mundane activities like walking somewhere or washing dishes or sipping tea, and involves becoming consciously and fully aware of your thoughts and actions in the present moment, non-judgmentally, existing in the moment.

When you are living 'in the moment', fully engaged in what you are doing, fully aware of the present moment, then you are existing in a state where there is no anger and there is no worry. By not dwelling on the past or speculating about the future, by embracing fully the present moment, you are living the precepts, and mindfulness brings with it humility, honesty, compassion and forgiveness.

So mindfulness is a way of experiencing Mikao Usui's spiritual principles.

(4) Work on yourself daily

Reiki isn't something that you can pick up once in a while, play around with for a bit, and then drop again… not if you are looking to receive the many benefits that are available from the system, anyway. If you are looking for consistent benefits then you need a consistent practice. The precepts say "just for today", and that is a good starting point: just do something with Reiki today. You can manage that. It doesn't have to be hours and hour's worth. Just do something for 10 minutes: you have ten minutes. Do something for 20 minutes. And if you don't have ten minutes, get up 10 minutes earlier: problem solved.

Don't worry about what you will do tomorrow: just focus on today.

When tomorrow comes, do the same. Just do something with Reiki, even for ten minutes. Don't worry about tomorrow: just do something today.

(5) Commitment is the key

There are spectacular benefits to be enjoyed through practising Reiki, and all you need to do is to work with the energy consistently, focus on the precepts and practise mindfulness. The benefits build up cumulatively, you see, and sporadic and occasional practice isn't enough if you want the very best out of your Reiki. You will get out of the system what you are prepared to put into it, so Reiki deserves a little of your time each day. You need to plug away at a few simple things, a few simple exercises or routines, and make them a regular part of your day, as regular a part of your routine as brushing your teeth or your hair.

And once you have established a regular habit of working on yourself with Reiki then you will find that it is difficult to stop: you will find that you really miss your hatsurei session or your self-treatment if you miss a day. That is the sort of position you are looking to get yourself into and by committing yourself to working with Reiki each day, even if it is a little inconvenient, you will reach that point.

(6) Don't try too hard

While we do need to commit ourselves and establish a decent routine of working on ourselves in order to obtain the many benefits that are available to us through Reiki, we should at the same time make sure that we do not try too hard, work for too long, or take our practice too seriously. Reiki is best enjoyed in a gentle, laid-back and light-hearted fashion rather than in a fists-clenched, furrowed-brow, tense, 'ready for a lot of hard work' sort of way. We do not force Reiki and we do not force a fierce practice on ourselves.

Reiki is rather like a flowing stream of water, and we are a rough rock sitting in that stream. The rock will become smooth, of course, but this will be achieved gently, through having the water flow consistently, and this will be done in its own time.

We might read about some of the experiences that other Reiki people might have when working on themselves, or receiving attunements/empowerments, or treating others (seeing colours, feeling particular things) and we may not notice all these things ourselves; we may notice very little. We may then think that if only we tried a bit harder then we would notice these things and then we would then be 'doing it properly'.

But trying hard and trying to force things is the best way there is to put a great big block on your progress. You will progress fastest when you give up trying and just be. Stand aside (metaphorically), do the exercises, treat people, and don't think or worry about what you do or do not experience. Be a bystander, be neutral and empty, have no expectations. That is the best approach, the approach that will lead you to progress at the right speed for you.

(7) You don't need to be perfect

Along with the need to be relaxed and laid-back and light-hearted about your practice, you should also make sure that you are not beating yourself up for not being perfect! You do not have to be perfect in order to obtain benefits for yourself through Reiki, or to treat other people successfully. No-one else is perfect, so you don't have to be either.

So perhaps your mind wanders when you do a treatment or work on yourself. So what? This happens to everybody else. Don't worry about it (there is something in the precepts about worrying). It you make a big thing about it and try through 'force of will' to have an empty mind, you have just made things worse: now you have two lots of thoughts… the first thoughts and then all the new thoughts about getting rid of the first lot of thoughts! Don't worry. Pay the thoughts no attention. Let them go. Bring your attention gently back to what you were doing. Feel the energy flowing through you; imagine yourself merging with the person on the treatment table. Over time your mind will settle, and you'll spend more of your time in a nice empty meditative state, but thoughts may well intrude again, and some days will probably be better than others. That's ok. You're human. It will sort itself out with time.

(8) Don't keep trying to puzzle out 'why'

To get the best out of your Reiki I recommend that you don't spend too much time trying to puzzle out why you are - or are not – experiencing a particular thing. Don't keep trying to work out what a particular colour that you or the recipient saw during a treatment means, or ponder the significance of a colour that you saw when self-treating. Don't keep wondering what a particular sensation in your hand means or why you felt a lot of energy flowing into a particular area of someone's body, or why you didn't feel any energy flowing into a particular place. It doesn't matter.

Your head can really mess up your experience of Reiki if you keep on frantically thinking about, analysing and questioning things. Don't think! Just be. Empty your mind, merge with the energy, if you are treating someone then merge with the recipient, and let it happen. Follow the flow of energy when you are treating, yes, and allow your hands to stay for longer in areas where more energy is coming through, but don't start frantically trying to puzzle out what is going on: Reiki works on lots of levels and you won't know what's happening so you may as well give up thinking about it and let go: enjoy the process, enjoy your treatments and give up the mental effort! It makes it so much easier that way!

(9) Trust your intuition

Along with not questioning everything that you feel or don't feel, you should also not keep on doubting the things that you are feeling and noticing. If you feel something, you feel it: you are not making it up. You cannot make yourself feel something.

So if you notice that energy is flowing into you more strongly in a particular area when you are self-treating, accept that and go with it, self-treating for longer there than in other positions. The same applies when treating someone else: if you feel that there is a 'hot spot' or 'fizzy area' then accept the sensations and treat for longer there. You are not making it up.

Neither are you making it up if you feel strangely drawn to a particular area of the body. You are intuitive and you can work intuitively straight away. All you need to do is to stop second-guessing and doubting yourself, be still, and simply accept what comes to you. It doesn't need to make sense. Don't try and puzzle it out: just accept it and treat in the way that feels appropriate.

(10) Ignore silly rules and restrictions

While we are making sure that we are not cluttering our practice with endless thoughts, questions and doubts, we should also thrown out as unnecessary the various rules, regulations and restrictions that we may have been taught. Reiki does not need to be controlled, blunted and restricted by man-made rules that have no basis. Reiki is safe and Reiki is simple, and simple approaches are usually the most effective.

So we do not have to slavishly follow a prescribed set of hand positions when treating ourselves or other people and we do not need to say a set form of words for our Reiki to work. We do not need to follow ritualised sets of hand and body movements in a particular sequence to be able to treat someone and we do not need to refrain from treating people with various medical conditions. Reiki is safe and Reiki is adaptable. It allows many different ways of working that are all valid. There is no 'one' way that Reiki has to be used, and we should ignore admonitions that we should 'always', or 'never', do a particular thing.

So, to get the most out of your Reiki, I recommend that you make a commitment to yourself to work on yourself each day as your top priority, but not beating yourself up if you miss the occasional day. Use Hatsurei ho and self-treat, focus on the precepts and drip-feed mindfulness into more and more of your daily activities. Don't try too hard though: be light-hearted and forgiving towards yourself because you don't have to be perfect. Try not to clutter your mind with lots of thoughts and doubts and questions: just be neutral, have no expectations, be empty and content. And make sure you keep it simple.

Notes

Notes

Notes

Notes

Lightning Source UK Ltd.
Milton Keynes UK
UKHW011928130119
335491UK00001B/22/P

9 780956 316868